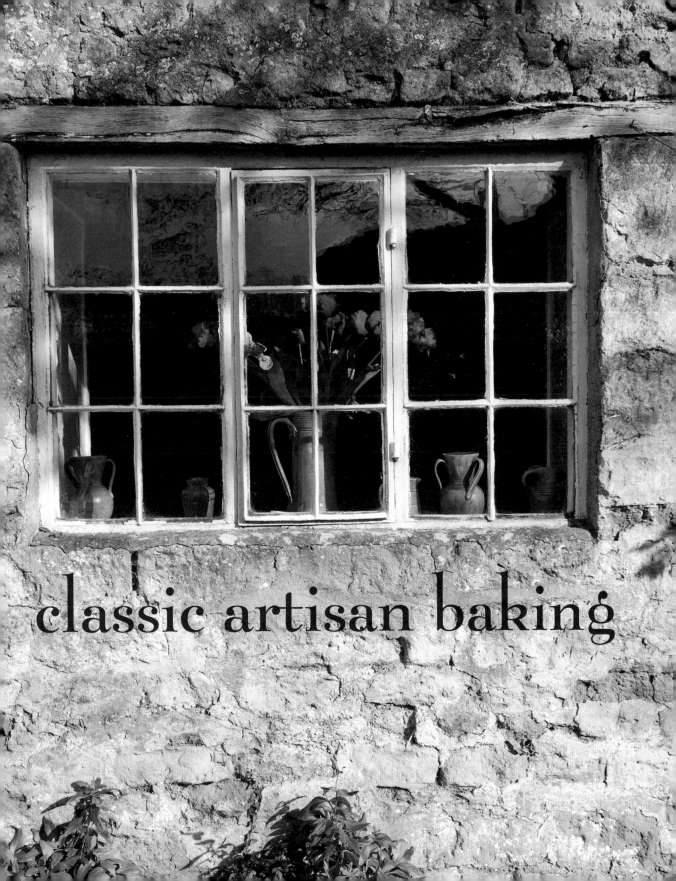

classic artisan baking

classic artisan baking

recipes for cakes, cookies, muffins and more

Julian Day

photography by Steve Painter

RYLAND
PETERS
& SMALL

LONDON NEW YORK

About the author

Julian Day ran his own food wholesaling business based in rural Warwickshire for many years. In 2001 he was approached by Meg's family to take over the mail-order bakery business of Meg Rivers Cakes. Establishing a new bakery in a converted barn near Shipston on Stour, he began production again, using the original Meg Rivers recipes. He lives in Chipping Campden, Gloucestershire and continues to run the business with the help of two of his four daughters.

About the photographer

Steve Painter worked for Ryland Peters & Small for ten years, designing, art directing photography and prop styling many of their cookery books, including the number 1 bestselling *The Hummingbird Bakery Cookbook*. Now freelance, he lives in the seaside town of Hastings where he designed and photographed this book. For Ryland Peters and Small he has also photographed *Whoopie Pies*, *How to Make Bread* and *Gelato*.

DESIGN, PHOTOGRAPHY AND PROP STYLING
Steve Painter
COMMISSIONING EDITOR Céline Hughes
HEAD OF PRODUCTION Patricia Harrington
ART DIRECTOR Leslie Harrington
EDITORIAL DIRECTOR Julia Charles

FOOD STYLIST Lucy Mckelvie
INDEXER Hilary Bird

Published in 2012 by
Ryland Peters & Small
20–21 Jockey's Fields
London WC1R 4BW
and
519 Broadway, 5th Floor
New York, NY 10012
www.rylandpeters.com

10 9 8 7 6 5 4 3 2 1

Text © Julian Day 2012
Design and photographs
© Ryland Peters & Small 2012

Printed in China

UK ISBN: 978 1 84975 196 4
US ISBN: 978 1 84975 225 1

A CIP record for this book is available from the British Library.

A CIP record for this book is available from the Library of Congress.

NOTES
- All spoon measurements are level, unless otherwise specified.
- Uncooked or partially cooked eggs should not be served to the very young, the very old, those with compromised immune systems, or to pregnant women.
- When a recipe calls for the grated zest of citrus fruit, buy unwaxed fruit and wash well before using. If you can only find treated fruit, scrub well in warm soapy water and rinse before using.
- Ovens should be preheated to the specified temperature. Recipes in this book were tested using a regular oven. If using a fan/convection oven, follow the manufacturer's instructions for adjusting temperatures.
- Small panettone cases (approximately 70 x 50 mm/3 x 2 inches), as used for the Mini-Meg recipes, can be bought from these online suppliers:
www.bakerybits.co.uk
www.beryls.com
www.amazon.co.uk
www.amazon.com

contents

Introduction

Most of us at one time or another have held a fantasy about turning our hobby into our living. While most of us only dream, Meg Rivers was someone who actually achieved this. I first met Meg when we were both living and working in the Warwickshire village of Upper Tysoe. Our children were of an age and they went to the local school together. We were each running our own small businesses, and we'd often chat about the problems and benefits of working for ourselves. Meg was already something of a celebrity, often appearing in the food pages of magazines, but more impressive to me was that she had the only fax machine in the village, which she let me use! Chatting in her tiny office with the fantastic scents of fruit cakes from the bakery beyond was always a pleasure.

I had no idea then that one day, I would be running the Meg Rivers Artisan Bakery.

Always a keen cook, Meg had learned to bake helping in her mother's tearooms in Bowral, in the Southern Tablelands of Australia. In the 1980s, she moved to the UK, married and set up home in rural Warwickshire. When she started a family, like many mums she became aware of her children's desire for sweet things but didn't want them to eat the kind of commercial cakes and baked goods available at the time. Having always been interested in healthy eating, Meg was particularly reluctant for her family to eat products made with artificial flavourings, colourings or preservatives.

Knowing that it was possible for treats to be both tasty and wholesome, she began baking at home, making the kind of things she'd enjoyed herself as a child. Family and friends raved about her baking and asked her to bake for them too. Gradually, her reputation grew, and when someone asked her to post a fruit cake to Africa, the idea of a mail-order bakery business was born.

In 1986, Meg found herself needing to provide an income for her family, something that she could fit around the demands of three young children. Starting small and working from her home kitchen, she began baking cakes and selling them mail-order. Her background in PR helped her gain publicity; in those pre-internet days, selling food mail-order was something of a rarity and a young woman juggling the difficulties of being a lone parent with running her own business was also rather unusual. The enterprise prospered and in 1991 she won the Businesswoman of the Year Award. This provided additional welcome publicity and a small cash prize, which Meg used to open a small bakery in Tysoe, Warwickshire.

Meg always insisted on using the best available ingredients and tried whenever possible to source things locally. More than 25 years later, though sadly Meg is no longer with us, we're still sticking to the same principles. At our bakery in the Cotswolds we often feel we have the best job in the world – we live and work in a beautiful part of the country, making lovely things for lovely people. I'm pretty sure this rural environment impacts on our working philosophy too. Maybe it's something to do with the slower pace of life in the countryside but we like to take the time required to o things properly. Yes, we live in the internet age when we all expect everything to be available 24/7 and it's true that our cakes are often made and despatched one day, to be with our customers at the other end of the country the next day. But we strongly believe in retaining an artisan approach. For us, the integrity of the recipe is vital and we won't ever compromise quality for the convenience.

We're a small team and we bake our cakes on a small scale, using the same low-tech, traditional methods that will be familiar to any home baker. In this book we've deliberately tried to keep the amount of equipment needed to a minimum – pretty much everything needed will be the type that most home kitchens will have. We love what we do and we want others to share the pleasure we get from baking. Our first ever recipe book will show that you don't need to be an expert to get great results. All the recipes are simple to follow and have been tried and tested by the Meg Rivers team. Many are exactly the same as the cakes we've been sending out to happy customers around the world since Meg first started her business. Some have been chosen from ones that are particularly popular with visitors to our café and shop in Chipping Campden, and others are simply personal favourites gathered from family and friends.

There's something to suit every occasion here; quick and easy teatime treats, tasty and nourishing family favourites and sophisticated dinner party desserts. There are so many reasons to get baking. Cakes are by their very nature a treat and treats are best shared. Meg began baking for her family and that's a great place to start – who better to spoil than those you love the most?

Baking is fun and the best results come from keeping things simple – don't take short cuts for the sake of convenience and take your time when baking; it's a wonderful way to chill out. Always use the best ingredients you can find – because that way even the humblest cake can be elevated to something rather special. There's always something magical about following a recipe; the alchemy of selecting, measuring and mixing the ingredients followed by the mysterious transformation of the baking process itself – and best of all, you get to eat the results!

Julian Day
Proprietor, Meg Rivers Artisan Bakery

family cakes

dundee cake

This almond fruit cake is Meg's version of an old Scottish recipe. Dundee cake was first sold commercially in the nineteenth century by Keiller's, a famous marmalade producer, as a way of keeping their staff busy when oranges were out of season. Lightly fruited and with a high ground-almond content, this is a lovely cut-and-come-again cake, ideal to eat at any time of year.

175 g/1½ sticks salted butter, soft

155 g/¾ cup (caster) sugar

4 eggs, lightly beaten

210 g/1⅓ cups ground almonds

140 g/1 generous cup plain/ all-purpose flour

365 g/2½ cups sultanas/golden raisins

115 g/¾ cup mixed candied peel

25 g/1 oz. crystallized ginger, chopped

24 blanched almonds, to decorate

18-cm/7-inch round cake pan, lined with baking parchment

Serves 10–12

Preheat the oven to 150°C (300°F) Gas 2.

Cream the butter and sugar together in a large bowl until pale and fluffy. Add the beaten eggs in 2 stages, stirring to a smooth batter each time. With a wooden spoon, fold in the ground almonds and flour, stirring until smooth. Add the sultanas/golden raisins, mixed candied peel and ginger and stir until evenly distributed.

Spoon the mixture into the prepared cake pan and smooth level with a palette knife. Decorate the top of the cake with the almonds. Bake in the preheated oven for about 2 hours – the cake will turn a good colour well before this, but be patient and test the middle with a skewer. Only when the skewer comes out clean is the cake ready. If it doesn't come out clean, give it another 5–10 minutes. The high ground-almond content in this recipe means there is often an oily, under-cooked appearance to the cake when first removed from the oven, but don't worry – the skewer does not lie and the oil will re-absorb into the cake on cooling!

This will keep for up to 14 days in an airtight container.

VARIATION: To make 8 Mini-Meg-style cakes, make the cake mixture as above, then divide between 8 small panettone cases (see page 4) and bake for 50–60 minutes, or until a skewer inserted in the middle comes out clean.

caraway seed cake

Perhaps this cake fell out of favour with a generation of schoolchildren who came to associate it with boring tea parties hosted by grim-faced maiden aunts. Maybe this delicately flavoured cake is more suited to adult tastes, but it is certainly overdue a revival.

195 g/13 tablespoons salted butter, soft

195 g/1 cup (caster) sugar

3 eggs

¼ teaspoon vanilla extract

145 g/1 cup plus 2 tablespoons plain/all-purpose flour

45 g/⅓ cup self-raising flour

50 g/⅓ cup ground almonds

2 teaspoons caraway seeds

15-cm/6-inch round cake pan, lined with baking parchment

Serves 8–10

Preheat the oven to 170°C (325°F) Gas 3.

Cream the butter and sugar together in a large bowl until pale and fluffy.

Crack the eggs into a small bowl and add the vanilla and ½ teaspoon water, lightly beating together. Add this in stages to the creamed butter, mixing thoroughly with a fork each time to obtain as smooth a blend as possible.

Add both flours and the ground almonds and fold into the mixture with a wooden spoon. Mix to a smooth consistency, then add the caraway seeds and stir till evenly distributed.

Spoon the mixture into the prepared cake pan and smooth level with a palette knife. Bake in the preheated oven for about 60–70 minutes. A skewer inserted in the middle should come out clean. Let cool for a few minutes, then turn the cake out onto a wire rack.

It tastes best when it is left to rest overnight in an airtight container, and it will keep for 2–3 days.

amaretto, date & pecan cake

Here's a cake that gets your taste buds going simply by the wonderful aroma it produces as it bakes. It's really worth finding fresh Medjool dates if you can. Sometimes described as 'the king of dates', they are exceptionally succulent and flavoursome and somehow help the subtle flavour of the Amaretto liqueur come to the fore.

150 g/1 cup plus 2 tablespoons plain/all-purpose flour

150 g/1 cup plus 2 tablespoons self-raising flour

170 g/¾ cup plus 2 tablespoons dark muscovado sugar

¼ teaspoon ground cinnamon

½ teaspoon baking powder

80 g/5 tablespoons salted butter

1½ tablespoons milk

1½ tablespoons Amaretto liqueur

¼ teaspoon almond extract

135 g/4½ oz. Medjool dates, pitted and chopped

40 g/¼ cup chopped pecans, to decorate

18-cm/7-inch round baking pan, lined with baking parchment

Serves 8

Preheat the oven to 180°C (350°F) Gas 4.

Combine both flours, the sugar, cinnamon and baking powder in a large bowl. Melt the butter in a small saucepan, then add it to the bowl of dry ingredients, followed by 150 ml/⅔ cup warm water, the milk, Amaretto and almond extract, stirring continually.

Add the chopped dates and stir until evenly distributed.

Spoon the mixture into the prepared cake pan and smooth level with a palette knife. Sprinkle the pecans evenly over the top. Bake in the preheated oven for about 50–55 minutes. A skewer inserted in the middle should come out clean. Let cool for a few minutes, then turn the cake out onto a wire rack.

It tastes best on the day of baking but it will keep in an airtight container for 2–3 days.

hazelnut & chocolate cake

This simple cake, based on an old Italian recipe, had one of the best responses ever from our Cake Club members. It's not difficult to understand why – the straightforward, no-nonsense combination of ground hazelnuts and chocolate works so well together. Just add a pot of tea or coffee, sit back and enjoy.

3 eggs

200 g/1 cup (caster) sugar

120 g/1 stick salted butter

40 g/1½ oz. dark/bittersweet chocolate, roughly chopped

150 g/1 cup plus 3 tablespoons plain/all-purpose flour

¼ teaspoon baking powder

120 g/1 scant cup ground hazelnuts (see Tip opposite)

handful of whole and broken hazelnuts, to decorate

18-cm/7-inch round cake pan, lined with baking parchment

Serves 8

Preheat the oven to 170°C (325°F) Gas 3.

Put the eggs, sugar and 4 tablespoons warm water in a large bowl and beat with a balloon whisk until smooth and no sugar granules remain at the bottom of bowl.

Put the butter and chocolate in a heatproof bowl over a saucepan of barely simmering water. Do not let the base of the bowl touch the water. Heat until melted, then stir until well mixed and glossy.

Add the melted butter and chocolate mixture to the bowl of beaten eggs, stirring gently until smooth. Add the flour, baking powder and ground hazelnuts and stir to a smooth paste.

Spoon the mixture into the prepared cake pan and smooth level with a palette knife. Sprinkle the whole and broken hazelnuts evenly over the top. Bake in the preheated oven for about 85–90 minutes. A skewer inserted in the middle should come out clean. Let cool for a few minutes, then turn the cake out onto a wire rack.

It tastes best on the day of baking but it will keep in an airtight container for 3–4 days.

TIP: If you can't find ground hazelnuts, buy whole blanched or finely chopped hazelnuts and grind in a food processor or coffee grinder.

VARIATION: To make 7 Mini-Meg-style cakes, make the cake mixture as above, then divide between 7 small panettone cases (see page 4) and bake for 35–40 minutes, or until a skewer inserted in the middle comes out clean.

st clement's cake

'Oranges and lemons say the bells of St Clement's' – so goes the old English nursery rhyme, so it's not difficult to guess the signature ingredients of this cake. With subtle undertones of orange liqueur, it's perfect for summer.

finely grated zest and freshly squeezed juice of 1 large orange

finely grated zest and freshly squeezed juice of 1 large lemon

55 g/¼ cup orange marmalade

35 g/¼ cup finely chopped mixed candied peel

2 teaspoons orange liqueur, such as Cointreau or Grand Marnier

160 g/11 tablespoons salted butter, soft

160 g/¾ cup (caster) sugar

3 eggs, lightly beaten

40 g/3 tablespoons ground almonds

120 g/1 cup plain/all-purpose flour

50 g/⅓ cup self-raising flour

candied citrus slices

200 g/1 cup granulated sugar

20 g/1½ tablespoons glucose syrup/liquid glucose

1 orange, sliced 7 mm/⅓ inch thick

1 lemon, sliced 7 mm/⅓ inch thick

8 small panettone cases (page 4)

Serves 8–10

To make the candied citrus slices, put the sugar, glucose and 40 ml/2½ tablespoons water in a large, stainless steel saucepan and slowly bring to the boil – do not stir. Remove from the heat and using metal tongs, place the fruit in the mixture, ensuring the pieces do not overlap. Over low heat, boil the fruit for about 15 minutes, turning 4 times to ensure even cooking. Let cool in the syrup, then shake off any excess syrup and let dry on waxed paper.

When you are ready to start making the cake, preheat the oven to 170°C (325°F) Gas 3.

Put the citrus zest and juice, marmalade, mixed peel and liqueur in a bowl, stir and let soak. Meanwhile, cream the butter and sugar together in a large bowl until pale and fluffy. Add the beaten eggs in 2 stages, stirring to a smooth batter each time. With a wooden spoon, fold in the ground almonds and both flours, stirring until smooth. Add the soaked fruit mixture and stir until evenly distributed. Spoon the mixture into the panettone cases and smooth level with a palette knife. Bake in the preheated oven for 35 minutes. Remove the cakes from the oven and place a candied citrus slice on each cake. Return to oven for a further 5–10 minutes. A skewer inserted in the middle of the cakes should come out clean. If they appear to be colouring too quickly, cover with baking parchment. Let cool on a wire rack. They will keep in an airtight container for 3–4 days, or can be frozen for up to 2 months.

VARIATION: To make 1 large cake, make the mixture as above, then spoon into a baking parchment-lined, 18-cm/7-inch round cake pan and bake for 40 minutes. Remove from the oven, place the candied citrus slices on top, then return to the oven for 15–20 minutes.

passion fruit & mango roulade

This roulade looks fabulous, tastes wonderful and is not as difficult to make as you might imagine.

3 eggs

140 g/¾ cup (caster) sugar,
plus extra to dust

¼ teaspoon vanilla extract

100 g/¾ cup plain/all-purpose
flour

icing/confectioners' sugar, to dust

filling

300 ml/1¼ cups whipping cream

2 tablespoons (caster) sugar

¼ teaspoon vanilla extract

2 passion fruit

1 mango, peeled and thinly sliced

*deep, 40 x 35-cm/16 x 14-inch
baking sheet, baselined with
baking parchment*

Serves 8–10

Preheat the oven to 220°C (425°F) Gas 7.

Whisk the eggs, sugar and vanilla to a thick and creamy consistency using an electric hand whisk. Remove the beaters and sift the flour onto the mixture. Using a balloon whisk, lift and twist the mixture, turning the bowl at the same time. You want to keep as much air in the mixture as possible, so do not over mix at this stage otherwise it can break down and become too soft. Scrape the mixture onto the prepared baking sheet and spread evenly with a palette knife, right to the edges. Bake for about 8–10 minutes or until pale golden and the surface springs back from light finger pressure. Lay a tea towel on a work surface and cover with a sheet of baking paper, then lightly dust the paper with (caster) sugar. Remove the cake from the oven and turn out onto the sugared paper. Immediately peel off the baking paper from the base of the cake before laying it back on top. Allow to cool until safe enough to handle. Roll the cake with both sheets of paper in place – this will make it easier to roll later.

To make the filling, put the cream, sugar and vanilla into a mixing bowl and whisk until firm-ish peaks are formed. Unroll the cake and discard the top sheet of paper. Spread the whipped cream evenly over the surface, leaving a narrow border around the edge to allow the filling to spread. Spread the passion fruit and mango on top of the cream. Starting with a longer edge furthest away from you, roll the cake towards you, pulling the paper on the base to keep it firm and tight. Transfer to serving a plate and dust icing/confectioners' sugar over the top. It tastes best on the day of baking but will keep, refrigerated, for 2–3 days.

lemon drizzle cake

This cake tastes first and foremost of lemon. There is no sugary-sweet icing, just a sharp syrup made with fresh lemons, drizzled over the cake still hot from the oven so that the lovely lemony flavour is absorbed right through. You will need to use a paper baking case to stop the syrup from seeping out of the cake.

200 g/1 stick plus 4 tablespoons salted butter, soft

170 g/¾ cup plus 1 tablespoon (caster) sugar

3 eggs, lightly beaten

65 g/⅔ cup ground almonds

130 g/1 cup plain/all-purpose flour

130 g/1 cup self-raising flour

finely grated zest and freshly squeezed juice of 1 large lemon

syrup

150 g/¾ cup (caster) sugar

freshly squeezed juice of 2 large lemons

18-cm/7-inch round cake pan, lined with an 18-cm/7-inch paper baking case

Serves 8

Preheat the oven to 170°C (325°F) Gas 3.

Cream the butter and sugar together in a large bowl until pale and fluffy. Add the beaten eggs in 3 stages, whisking until smooth. Fold in the ground almonds, flours, lemon zest and juice.

Spoon the mixture into the prepared cake pan. Bake in the preheated oven for 50 minutes. A skewer inserted in the middle should come out clean.

Meanwhile, to make the syrup, bring 3 tablespoons water, the sugar and lemon juice slowly to the boil in a pan, stirring all the time, until the sugar has dissolved.

With the hot cake still in the pan, pierce the cake to about three-quarters of its depth with a skewer, creating holes about 2 cm/1 inch apart all over the cake. Slowly pour the syrup all over the surface and allow it to soak in. Let cool in the pan before serving.

The cake will keep for 5 days in an airtight container and can be frozen for up to 2 months.

victoria sponge

There's something timeless and delightful about this classic English cake. A childhood favourite with so many people, adding ripe strawberries or other seasonally available fresh, soft fruit lifts it to another level.

150 g/1¼ sticks salted butter, soft

150 g/¾ cup (caster) sugar

3 eggs, lightly beaten

150 g/1 cup plus 2 tablespoons self-raising flour, sifted

filling

60 g/4 tablespoons salted butter, soft

125 g/¾ cup plus 2 tablespoons icing/confectioners' sugar, plus extra to dust

¼ teaspoon vanilla extract

4 tablespoons strawberry jam

8–10 strawberries, hulled and halved (optional)

deep, 18-cm/7-inch round cake pan, baselined with baking parchment

Serves 8–10

Preheat the oven to 180°C (350°F) Gas 4.

Cream the butter and sugar together in a large bowl until pale and fluffy. Add the beaten eggs in 3 batches, whisking until smooth. Fold in the flour.

Spoon the mixture into the prepared cake pan. Bake in the preheated oven for 45–50 minutes. A skewer inserted in the middle should come out clean. When ready, the sides of the cake will come away from the pan and the top will spring back from light finger pressure. Remove from the oven and turn out onto a wire rack to cool.

When the cake has completely cooled, slice it in half horizontally. The best way to do this is to lay a hand on top of the cake to hold it firmly in place. With a long-bladed, serrated knife, slice the cake, drawing the knife towards you. Repeat this action, turning the cake and using the first cut as a guide.

To make the filling, put the butter, sugar, 3 teaspoons warm water and the vanilla extract into a bowl and beat with an electric hand whisk. Start slowly, then increase the speed until the mixture is as light and white as possible. Spread the filling onto the cut side of the bottom half of the cake. If using strawberries, arrange some of them over the filling. Spread the jam onto the cut side of the top of the cake, then carefully sandwich the 2 halves together. Dust with icing/confectioners' sugar and decorate with more strawberries, if using.

The cake will keep for 7 days in an airtight container and can be frozen (without the filling) for up to 2 months.

ginger cake

Year after year, this is one of our best-selling cakes. It has a warm golden colour and a pleasant spicy flavour with just the right amount of sweetness – just the thing to enjoy with a cup of tea on a winter's day.

250 g/8½ oz. crystallized ginger, diced

3 tablespoons ginger wine

150 g/1¼ sticks salted butter, soft

100 g/½ cup (caster) sugar

3 eggs

70 g/½ cup ground almonds

2 tablespoons ground ginger

150 g/1 cup plain/all-purpose flour

50 g/⅔ cup self-raising flour

18-cm/7-inch round cake pan, lined with baking parchment

Serves 8–10

Preheat the oven to 150°C (300°F) Gas 2.

Put 200 g/6½ oz. of the crystallized ginger into a bowl and pour the ginger wine over it. Allow to soak.

In a large mixing bowl, cream the butter and sugar together until pale and fluffy. Add the eggs one at a time, beating between each addition. Add the ground almonds and ginger, flours and soaked crystallized ginger and stir well.

Spoon the mixture into the prepared cake pan, smooth level with a palette knife and top with the remaining crystallized ginger. Bake in the preheated oven for about 80 minutes. A skewer inserted in the middle should come out clean. Remove from the oven and turn out onto a wire rack to cool. The cake will keep for 7–10 days in an airtight container.

VARIATION: To make 7 Mini-Meg-style cakes, make the cake mixture as above, then divide between 7 small panettone cases (see page 4) and bake for 40 minutes, or until a skewer inserted in the middle comes out clean.

coffee & walnut cake

Always popular at our café, this straightforward cake seems to be a particular favourite with our male customers. It's simple to make and the subtle flavour of the walnuts combines so well with the rich coffee tones to make a delicious cake that tastes as good as it looks.

1 tablespoon instant coffee powder

2 tablespoons water, boiling

100 g/¾ cup plain/all-purpose flour

100 g/¾ cup self-raising flour

170 g/1½ sticks salted butter, soft

150 g/¾ cup (caster) sugar

3 eggs

55 g/⅓ cup ground almonds

100 g/⅔ cup walnuts, chopped, plus
   12 walnut halves, to decorate

filling

1 tablespoon instant coffee powder

2 tablespoons water, boiling

150 g/1¼ sticks salted butter, soft

300 g/2 cups icing/confectioners' sugar

*deep, 18-cm/7-inch round cake pan,
   lined with baking parchment*

Serves 8–10

Preheat the oven to 170°C (325°F) Gas 3.

In a cup, mix the coffee powder and boiling water until smooth and well mixed. Sift together both flours and set aside. In a large bowl, cream the butter and sugar together until pale and fluffy. Add the eggs one at a time, beating between each addition. Add the coffee, followed by the sifted flours, ground almonds and chopped walnuts. Stir together but do not over beat the mixture.

Spoon the mixture into the prepared cake pan, smooth level and bake in middle of the preheated oven for 55–60 minutes or until top of the cake springs back from light finger pressure and a skewer inserted into the middle of the cake comes out clean. Remove the cake from oven and let cool in the pan. Leave the oven on.

Place the walnut halves on a baking sheet and roast on the bottom shelf of the oven for 10 minutes. Remove from the oven and allow to cool.

To make the filling, mix the coffee powder and boiling water in a mixing bowl until smooth and well mixed. Allow to cool, then add the butter and sugar and beat together to a light, creamy texture.

When the cake is cool, turn it out of the pan and place on a flat surface. Lay a hand on top of the cake to hold it firmly in place. With a long-bladed, serrated knife, slice the cake, drawing the knife towards you. Repeat this action, turning the cake and using the first cut as a guide. Spread half the filling onto the cut side of the bottom half, then sandwich the 2 halves together. Coat the top of cake with the remaining filling and decorate with the roasted walnut halves. The cake will keep for 4–5 days in an airtight container.

chocolate cake

We first introduced this cake ten years ago and since then it's become such a favourite with our customers that it is now one of our top selling cakes. Rich, dark and moist without being cloying or overly sweet, the subtle undertones of coffee enhance the flavour of the chocolate. It works equally well without the ganache filling, which is how we send it out mail-order.

140 g golden syrup/light corn syrup

100 g/6½ tablespoons salted butter

100 g/½ cup (caster) sugar

2 tablespoons instant coffee powder

5 tablespoons water, boiling

2 tablespoons unsweetened cocoa powder

1 egg

2 tablespoons corn oil

230 g/1¾ cups plain/all-purpose flour

1 tablespoon bicarbonate of soda/baking soda

155 g/1 cup dark chocolate chips or finely diced dark chocolate (minimum 40% cocoa solids)

ganache filling

300 g/10 oz. dark chocolate, finely chopped

100 g/6½ tablespoons salted butter

2 drops vanilla extract

120 g/½ cup single/light cream

18-cm/7-inch round cake pan, lined with baking parchment

Serves 8–10

Preheat the oven to 170°C (325°F) Gas 3.

Put the syrup and butter in a saucepan and and stir until just melted. Transfer to a large bowl, add the sugar and stir. In a cup, mix the coffee with the boiling water, then stir into the butter and syrup mixture. In a separate bowl, whisk together the cocoa powder and 4 tablespoons cold water, then stir into the mix. In another bowl, beat together the egg and oil and add to the mixture. Sift the flour and bicarbonate of soda/baking soda into the mixture, add the chocolate chips and stir everything together well.

Spoon the mixture into the prepared cake pan. Bake in the preheated oven for 75–85 minutes. A skewer inserted in the middle should come out clean. The cake may need to be covered with baking parchment for last 10 minutes if it looks like it is browning too much. Remove from the oven and turn out onto a wire rack to cool.

When the cake has completely cooled, slice it in half horizontally. Lay a hand on top of the cake to hold it firmly in place. With a long-bladed, serrated knife, slice the cake, drawing the knife towards you. Repeat this action, turning the cake and using the first cut as a guide.

To make the ganache filling, put the chocolate, butter and vanilla extract into a heatproof bowl. In a small saucepan, bring the cream to the boil, then pour it over the chocolate mixture, stirring until the chocolate has melted and the mixture is smooth. Allow to cool, stirring occasionally, then refrigerate. Check regularly and as soon as it shows signs of forming a soft, setting consistency, remove from the fridge and beat until lighter in colour. Use the ganache immediately, as it sets quickly. Spread the ganache over the cut side of the bottom half, then sandwich the 2 halves together. Alternatively, you can spread the ganache more sparingly in the middle and use the remaining ganache to cover the top of the cake.

The cake will keep for 7–10 days in an airtight container.

cherry cake

400 g/2⅔ cups whole glacé
  cherries, washed and drained,
  plus 10 to decorate

2 tablespoons Kirsch

150 g/1¼ sticks salted butter, soft

120 g/⅔ cup (caster) sugar

2 eggs

2 tablespoons corn oil

75 g/⅔ cup self-raising flour

120 g/1 scant cup plain/
  all-purpose flour

75 g/½ cup ground almonds

35 g/¼ cup finely chopped
  almonds

*15-cm/6-inch round cake pan,
lined with baking parchment*

Serves 6–8

There's something so cheerful about this colourful cake. It seems to bring a bit of summer sunshine to the table at any time of year. This is a recipe that truly does benefits from sourcing the best quality ingredients – we use naturally coloured glacé cherries from Provence in Southern France – so much better than those artificially bright red cherries found in commercial cakes.

Preheat the oven to 150°C (300°F) Gas 2.

Put the cherries in a bowl with the Kirsch and set aside to marinate.

In a large bowl, cream the butter and sugar together until pale and fluffy. Add the eggs one at a time, beating between each addition, then stir in the corn oil. Add the flours and the ground and chopped almonds and fold together, then add the marinated cherries and stir into the mixture.

Spoon the mixture into the prepared cake pan and bake in the preheated oven for 60 minutes. Remove from the oven, taking care not to jolt the cake, and top with the remaining 10 cherries. Return to the oven and bake for a further 20 minutes. A skewer inserted in the middle should come out clean. Remove from the oven and allow to stand for 30 minutes before turning out onto a wire rack to cool completely.

The cake will keep for 7 days in an airtight container.

VARIATION: To make 8 Mini-Meg-style cakes, make the cake mixture as above, then divide between 8 small panettone cases (see page 4) and bake for 40–45 minutes, or until a skewer inserted in the middle comes out clean.

lemon polenta cake

Polenta flour gives cakes a wonderful yellow colour with a pleasing grainy texture, and has the added bonus of being suitable for those with an intolerance to wheat flour. Fresh lemon juice and zest act as a nice counterpoint to the dense, buttery flavour of this cake.

2 large lemons

220 g/15 tablespoons salted butter, soft

220 g/1 cup plus 2 tablespoons (caster) sugar

4 eggs, lightly beaten

190 g/1⅓ cups ground almonds

125 g/1 cup polenta/cornmeal

1½ teaspoons baking powder

18-cm/7-inch round cake pan, baselined with baking parchment

Serves 8

Preheat the oven to 170°C (325°F) Gas 3.

Grate the zest from both lemons, and squeeze the juice from just one.

In a large bowl, cream the butter and sugar together until pale and fluffy. Add the eggs one at a time, beating between each addition, then stir in the lemon juice and zest, followed by the ground almonds, polenta/cornmeal and baking powder.

Spoon the mixture into the prepared cake pan, smooth level with a palette knife and bake in the preheated oven for 80–90 minutes. A skewer inserted in the middle should come out clean. Remove from the oven and allow to stand for a while. When cool enough to handle, run a knife around the inside of the pan and turn out onto a wire rack to cool completely.

The cake will keep for 4–5 days in an airtight container.

chocolate & hazelnut torte

This dark and creamy cake makes an ideal dinner-party dessert. Ground hazelnuts bring a sophisticated flavour that combines perfectly with dark chocolate. As there is no flour in this recipe, even those with an intolerance to wheat can enjoy it.

100 g/⅔ cup whole, blanched hazelnuts

250 g/8½ oz. dark/bittersweet chocolate, roughly chopped

100 g/7 tablespoons salted butter

6 eggs, separated

½ teaspoon cream of tartar

120 g/⅔ cup (caster) sugar

topping

200 g/6½ oz. dark/bittersweet chocolate, roughly chopped

125 g/1 stick salted butter

4 tablespoons whole, blanched hazelnuts

23-cm/9-inch round, loose-based cake pan, lined with baking parchment

Serves 10–12

Preheat the oven to 170°C (325°F) Gas 3.

Toast the hazelnuts for both the cake and the topping in the preheated oven for 10 minutes. Keep any eye on them to make sure they are not burning. Allow to cool, then set aside the 4 tablespoons for the topping and grind the remaining nuts to a fine powder in a food processor.

Melt the chocolate and butter in a heatproof bowl set over a pan of barely simmering water. Do not let the base of the bowl touch the water. Let cool.

In a bowl, beat the egg yolks together with a balloon whisk or electric hand whisk for about 2 minutes, or until they become pale in colour.

In a separate large bowl, and with a clean whisk or beaters, beat the egg whites and cream of tartar together until soft peaks are formed. Add the sugar in stages, beating continually, until stiff peaks are formed.

Add the beaten egg yolks to the melted butter and chocolate mixture and whisk lightly. Add half the egg whites to this mixture and gently fold together with a spatula. Transfer this mixture to the bowl with the remaining egg whites, add the ground hazelnuts and gently fold everything together.

Spoon the mixture into the prepared cake pan and bake in the preheated oven for 50 minutes or until the sides of the torte come away from the pan, and a skewer inserted into the middle of the torte comes out clean. Allow to cool completely before removing from the pan.

To make the topping, melt the chocolate and butter together as described above. Add 2 tablespoons warm water and stir until smooth. Remove the bowl from the pan and allow to cool. Spread over the top of the torte using a palette knife. Roughly chop the reserved roasted hazelnuts and sprinkle them over the middle of the torte, to decorate.

The torte will keep for 5–7 days in an airtight container, although it is best eaten within a day or two of baking.

simnel cake

This fantastic fruit cake was originally baked by servant girls for Mother's Day, but over time has become associated with Easter. Marzipan is the star in here – as well as the decoration, there is a layer inside the cake. Use the best natural marzipan you can find – the superior taste is worth the extra trouble.

130 g/1 stick plus 1 tablespoon salted butter, soft

100 g/½ cup dark muscovado/dark brown sugar

3 eggs

120 g/1 cup plain/all-purpose flour

1 teaspoon ground cinnamon

½ teaspoon freshly grated nutmeg

50 g/⅓ cup ground almonds

80 g/½ cup mixed candied peel

170 g/1¼ cups sultanas/golden raisins

170 g/1¼ cups Zante currants

100 g/⅔ cup whole glacé cherries, washed, drained and quartered

150 g/5 oz. natural marzipan

topping

200 g/6½ oz. natural marzipan

2 tablespoons apricot jam

15-cm/6-inch round cake pan, lined with baking parchment

chef's blowtorch (optional)

Serves 12–14

Preheat oven to 130°C (250°F) Gas ½.

In a large bowl, cream the butter and sugar together until paler and fluffy. Add the eggs one at a time, beating between each addition. Sift the flour, cinnamon and nutmeg together, then fold into the mix with the ground almonds. Add the mixed peel, sultanas/golden raisins, currants and glacé cherries and stir everything together.

Spoon half of the mixture into the prepared cake pan and level the surface.

Roll out the 150 g/5 oz. marzipan to about 5 mm/¼ inch thick and cut out a 12-cm/5-inch round disc. Place the disc on top of the cake mixture in the pan and spoon the remaining mixture over it. Smooth level with a palette knife and bake in the preheated oven for 2 hours. A skewer inserted in the middle of the cake should come out clean. Remove from the oven and allow to cool in the pan. When cool, remove from the pan and peel off the lining paper.

For the topping, take two-thirds of the marzipan and roll a second disc as described above. Boil the apricot jam, then brush it over the top of the cake and place the disc on top, smoothing down firmly. Crimp the edges of the marzipan between your thumb and index finger to create a fluted effect.

Roll out the remaining marzipan to form a rope 2 cm/1 inch in diameter. Divide into 11 equal pieces and roll into balls. Place them evenly around the edge of the cake, fixing with a spot of apricot jam. Lightly toast the top of the cake with a chef's blowtorch, or place under a hot grill/broiler about 10 cm/4 inches from the heat. Watching carefully (it's disappointing to set fire to the cake at this stage!), toast the surface for about 30 seconds, or until the desired colour is obtained. (See page 7 for a photograph of the cake browned all over.)

The cake will keep for 3–4 months in an airtight container.

wheat-free rich fruit cake

The first cake Meg sent by mail-order was her Rich English Fruit Cake, still one of our most popular cakes. This is our wheat-free version of the same recipe. Apart from the lack of gluten, making the cake a little crumblier when sliced, it is every bit as good – rich, moist and delicious. It is ideal as a Christmas cake that even those with an intolerance to wheat can enjoy. Make it in September, double-wrap in film and seal in an airtight container ready to enjoy, fully matured, in December.

115g/¾ cup Zante currants

115g/¾ cup sultanas/golden raisins

70 g/½ cup mixed candied peel

60 g/½ cup chopped glacé cherries

25 g/3 tablespoons chopped crystallized ginger

45 g/⅓ cup chopped walnuts

20 ml/4 teaspoons brandy

120 g/1 stick unsalted butter, soft

80 g/⅓ cup packed dark muscovado/dark brown sugar

2 medium eggs

90 g/⅔ cup wheat-free plain flour

35 g/¼ cup ground almonds

1 teaspoon ground mixed spice/apple pie spice

¼ teaspoon ground cloves

topping

9 walnut halves

8 whole glacé cherries

deep, 15-cm/6-inch round cake pan, lined with baking parchment

Serves 8

Start the cake 2 days before you want to bake it.

Put the currants, sultanas/golden raisins, mixed peel, glacé cherries, ginger and chopped walnuts in a bowl. Add the brandy, cover with clingfilm/plastic wrap and allow to soak overnight.

The next day, preheat oven to 130°C (250°F) Gas ½.

In a large bowl, cream the butter and sugar together until paler and fluffy. Add the eggs one at a time, beating between each addition. Add the flour, ground almonds and spices and slowly fold in until a smooth mixture is obtained. Add the brandy-soaked fruits and stir in.

Spoon the mixture into the prepared cake pan and spread level with a palette knife. Decorate the top of the cake with the walnut halves and whole glacé cherries, placing them in a circular pattern.

Bake the cake in the middle of the preheated oven for about 90 minutes. A skewer inserted into the middle of the cake should come out clean. (The cake will remain soft to the touch when baked, unlike a pound cake that will spring back when pressed with your fingertips. The finished colour is not very different from the uncooked state and there will often be a residue of nut oil on the surface, but don't worry, the oil is absorbed back into the cake on cooling.) Remove from the oven and allow to stand for an 2 or two before turning out onto a wire rack to cool completely.

Allow the cake to set for 24 hours before serving. The longer you can leave it to mature, the better. Cut with a sharp serrated knife using a sawing motion.

The cake will keep for 6–8 weeks in an airtight container.

christmas pudding

The Sunday before Advent is traditionally known as 'Stir up Sunday'. This is the day when all the family gathered to make their Christmas pudding and everyone would stir it for good luck. But for me, the end of November is too late – make your pudding at least a couple of months in advance of eating it to allow the flavour to mature fully.

100 g/⅔ cup raisins

100 g/⅔ cup sultanas/golden raisins

100 g/⅔ cup Zante currants

75 g/½ cup mixed candied peel

30 g/3 tablespoons diced crystallized ginger

20 g/2 tablespoons walnut pieces

grated zest and juice of ½ orange

grated zest and juice of ½ lemon

5 tablespoons brandy

60 g/⅔ cup peeled and diced Bramley apple

1 egg, lightly beaten

50 g/⅓ cup plain/all-purpose flour

100 g/½ cup dark muscovado/dark brown sugar

50 g/½ cup wholemeal/whole-wheat breadcrumbs

70 g/2½ oz. vegetable suet, roughly chopped

1 tablespoon ground mixed spice/apple pie spice

¼ teaspoon ground cinnamon

¼ teaspoon freshly grated nutmeg

¼ teaspoon ground cloves

2-pint/4-cup pudding basin

circle of baking parchment to fit pudding basin

30-cm/12-inch square of muslin/cheesecloth

Serves 8

Start the pudding the day before you want to cook it.

Put the dried fruit, crystallized ginger, walnuts and citrus zest and juice into a large bowl. Pour the brandy over everything, cover with clingfilm/plastic wrap and allow to soak overnight.

The next day, add the diced apple and beaten egg to the brandy-soaked fruit and nuts and stir. Add the flour, sugar, breadcrumbs, suet and all the spices and stir thoroughly.

Spoon the mixture into the pudding basin, spread level with a palette knife and cover the mixture with the circle of baking parchment. Put the basin in the middle of the muslin/cheesecloth square, bring the corners together and tie in a loose double knot. Half-fill a large saucepan with boiling water, place the pudding basin in the saucepan and cover with the lid. Steam over low heat for 4 hours. Make sure you check the water level regularly and top up with boiling water as required. Do not allow to boil dry.

Remove the saucepan from the heat and carefully lift out the basin. If eating the day it is made, let the pudding stand for 15 minutes before serving.

If storing, remove the muslin square from around the basin. Let cool completely, then wrap 2 layers of clingfilm/plastic wrap around the entire basin and store in a cool, dry place. The pudding will keep for 6–9 months if stored in this way. I recommend maturing for at least 3 months.

festival cake

This spectacular-looking cake is surprisingly simple to make, with most of the effort being in preparing the fruit and nuts for overnight soaking. Delicious and impressive, it is a generously-sized cake that will take pride of place at any special occasion.

150 g/1 cup mixed candied peel

150 g/1 cup organic dried apricots, roughly chopped

450 g/3 cups sultanas/golden raisins

250 g/8½ oz. crystallized pineapple, chopped

130 g/4½ oz. crystallized ginger, chopped

250 g/1¾ cups whole glacé cherries, assorted colours, roughly chopped

160 ml/⅔ cup brandy

200 g/13 tablespoons salted butter, soft

160 g/¾ cup light muscovado/light brown sugar

6 eggs

360 g/2¾ cups plain/all-purpose flour

150 g/1 cup chopped pecans

260 g/2 cups chopped Brazil nuts

topping

75 g/½ cup organic dried apricots

100 g/⅔ cup whole glacé cherries, assorted colours

30 g/3 tablespoons whole blanched almonds

50 g/⅓ cup pecan halves

3 tablespoons apricot jam (optional)

empty 400-g/14-oz. can (such as a baked bean can)

23-cm/9-inch round, loose-based cake pan, lined with baking parchment

Serves 24

Start the cake the day before you want to bake it.

Put the mixed peel, chopped apricots, sultanas/golden raisins, crystallized pineapple and ginger and chopped cherries into a large bowl. Pour the brandy over everything, cover with clingfilm/plastic wrap and allow to soak overnight.

The next day, preheat the oven to 150°C (300°F) Gas 2.

Thoroughly clean the empty can and peel the label away. Line the outside of the can with baking parchment and place it in the middle of the prepared baking pan, open side up, to make a ring shape.

In a large bowl, cream the butter and muscovado sugar together until pale and fluffy. Add the eggs one at a time, beating between each addition – don't worry if the mixture curdles. Fold in the flour, then add the chopped nuts and soaked fruits and mix to an even consistency.

Spoon the mixture into the prepared cake pan and level the top. Top with the whole apricots, cherries, almonds and pecans. Bake in the preheated oven for about 90 minutes. A skewer inserted in the middle of the cake should come out clean. You may need to cover the cake with baking parchment towards the end of cooking if the fruits are browning too much.

Remove the cake from the oven and allow to cool completely in the pan. When cool, gently twist the can and remove, then turn the cake out onto a wire rack. If you would like a glossy appearance, boil the apricot jam, then brush it over the fruit and nut decoration.

The cake will keep for 2–3 months in an airtight container.

panforte

This delicious Italian dessert – part spicy fruit cake,
part honey and nut cookie – makes a wonderful
alternative to traditional Christmas cake. Full of
festive flavours and with a lovely chewy texture, it's
best served thinly sliced with coffee at the end of
your meal. Wrapped in baking parchment and tied
with string, it makes a delightful gift.

2 x 12.5-cm/5-inch edible wafer
  paper discs
50 g/⅓ cup whole blanched
  almonds
50 g/⅓ cup whole pistachios
50 g/⅓ cup whole hazelnuts
90 g/⅔ cup dried figs, stalks
  removed, and roughly chopped
1½ tablespoons sherry
5 tablespoons honey
75 g/⅓ cup (caster) sugar
40 g/⅓ cup plain/all-purpose flour
100 g/⅔ cup mixed candied peel
½ teaspoon ground cinnamon
1 teaspoon cardamom seeds,
  crushed
1 teaspoon freshly grated nutmeg
a pinch of ground cloves
icing/confectioners' sugar, to dust

*15-cm/6-inch shallow, round cake
pan, greased*

Serves about 16

Preheat the oven to 180°C (350°F) Gas 4.

Place an edible wafer disc in the bottom of the prepared cake pan.

Spread all the nuts onto a baking sheet and toast in the preheated for 10–15 minutes or until golden brown. Keep any eye on them to make sure they are not burning. Remove from the oven and place in the a clean, thick tea towel. Pull the towel up around them and twist tightly to enclose them. Vigorously rub the nuts through the towel until most of the skins are removed. Remove the nuts and discard the skins.

Put the dried figs in a food processor with the sherry, honey and sugar and blitz for 20 seconds. Transfer to a large saucepan and boil gently for about 6–8 minutes. Remove the saucepan from the heat and add the flour, mixed peel, spices and roasted nuts and stir well.

Spoon the mixture into the prepared baking pan and press down firmly (a slightly smaller pan wrapped in clingfilm/plastic wrap is handy for this). Place the second edible wafer disc on top of the cake and leave overnight to set. Dust icing/confectioners' sugar generously over the top before serving.

The cake will keep for up to 2 months in the refrigerator.

small cakes

rock cakes

I remember my sister bringing these home from 'domestic science' classes; hers were rather solid, but done properly, they are delicious.

250 g/2 cups plain/all-purpose flour

2 teaspoons baking powder

30 g/2 tablespoons salted butter

30 g/2½ tablespoons white vegetable shortening

50 g/⅓ cup mixed candied peel

60 g/⅓ cup (caster) sugar

50 g/⅓ cup sultanas/golden raisins

50 g/⅓ cup Zante currants

2 eggs

5 tablespoons milk

1 tablespoon demerara sugar

baking sheet lined with baking parchment

Makes 12

Preheat the oven to 200°C (400°F) Gas 6.

Sift the flour and baking powder into a large bowl. Dice the butter and vegetable shortening, add to the bowl and rub together using your fingertips to a fine crumb texture. Finely chopped the mixed peel to the same size as the raisins. Add the sugar and dried fruit and stir together.

In a separate bowl, lightly beat the eggs and milk together, then add to the flour mixture and blend to a firm-ish dough. You want a soft but not sticky or dry mixture, so if a bit dry, add a splash more milk.

Using 2 dessertspoons, shape the mixture into 12 rough mounds on the prepared baking sheet. Sprinkle the demerara sugar over the top. Bake in the middle of the preheated oven for 15 minutes or until the edges of the cakes turn a pale golden brown colour. Transfer the cakes to a wire rack to cool.

The cakes are best eaten on the day they're baked, but will keep for 24 hours in an airtight container.

plain & fruit scones

There are few things nicer than coming home to a plate full of freshly made scones. Quick and easy to make, plain or fruit, served warm or cold they are the quintessential English teatime treat. Spread with butter and your favourite jam, or push the boat out and add clotted cream and fresh fruit for the full 'cream tea' effect.

175 g/1⅓ cups plus 1 tablespoon bread flour

150 g/1 cup plus 3 tablespoons plain/all-purpose flour (See Tip below)

1 teaspoon baking powder

60 g/½ stick salted butter

75 g/⅓ cup (caster) sugar

120 ml/½ cup milk

2 eggs

1 egg, lightly beaten, to glaze

baking sheet lined with baking parchment

5-cm/2-inch round cookie cutter

Makes 15–20

Preheat the oven to 220°C (425°F) Gas 7.

Sift the flours and baking powder into a large mixing bowl. Add the butter and rub together with your fingers to achieve a fine crumb texture, then stir in the sugar.

In a separate bowl, whisk the 2 eggs and milk together. Add three-quarters of the egg mixture to the dry ingredients. Quickly beat all the ingredients together, adding extra egg mixture if necessary, to give a soft dough.

Turn the dough out onto a well-floured surface, work the dough into a ball, then roll it out until about 2 cm/1 inch thick. Use the cookie cutter to stamp out scones and place them on the prepared baking sheet. Re-roll any leftover dough and cut out scones, as before, until all the dough is used up. Brush the tops with the egg glaze.

Bake in the preheated oven for 12–15 minutes or until pale golden brown. Transfer to a wire rack to cool. Eat or freeze the same day.

Tip: We use strong bread flour in this recipe to help maintain height and shape during baking. If you don't have any to hand, using plain/all-purpose flour will work too.

Variation: For fruit scones, add 80 g/½ cup sultanas/golden raisins at the same time as you stir in the sugar.

chocolate & pecan muffins

Whereas cupcakes are probably just a passing fad, so often a disappointing triumph of style over substance, surely there will always be a place for muffins. Dark, glossy and inviting, this moist and nutty chocolate version is quick to make and freezes well, so you need never be short of the kind of cake that gave rise to the term 'comfort food'.

260 g/2 cups plain/all-purpose flour

1 tablespoon baking powder

a pinch of salt

60 g/½ cup unsweetened cocoa powder

100 g/⅔ cup roughly chopped pecans

180 g/scant cup (caster) sugar

150 g/1 cup dark/bittersweet chocolate chips

180 ml/¾ cup corn oil

2 eggs

210 ml/¾ cup plus 2 tablespoons milk

1 teaspoon vanilla extract

12-hole muffin pan, lined with paper cases

Makes 12

Preheat the oven to 190°C (375°F) Gas 5.

Put flour, baking powder, salt, cocoa powder, pecans, sugar and chocolate chips in a large bowl. In a separate bowl, whisk together the corn oil, eggs, milk and vanilla extract, then pour onto the dry ingredients. Beat all the ingredients together until just smooth.

Spoon the mixture into the paper cases, filling three-quarters full. Bake in the preheated oven for 25–30 minutes or until well risen and a skewer inserted into the middle of a muffin comes out clean. Remove from the oven and transfer to a wire rack and allow to cool slightly.

The muffins are best served slightly warm, but they will keep for up to 4 days in an airtight container. They can be frozen for up to 2 months.

madeleines

These lovely little cakes, shaped like scallop shells, are believed to have originated in the Lorraine region of France. Since Marcel Proust gave them a mention in his novel 'Remembrance of Things Past', generations of French children have come home from school to a plate of these to dip in their 'chocolat chaud'. They work equally well with a nice cup of tea or coffee.

130 g/1 cup plain/all-purpose flour
½ teaspoon baking powder
a pinch of salt
120 g/⅔ cup (caster) sugar
3 eggs
2 teaspoons honey
grated zest of 1 lemon
120 g/1 stick salted butter, melted and
    cooled
1 tablespoon icing/confectioners' sugar,
    to decorate

*non-stick madeleine pan, buttered and
    floured*

Makes about 24

Preheat the oven to 190°C (375°F) Gas 5.

Sift the flour, baking powder and salt into a bowl and set aside.

In a large bowl, whisk the sugar, eggs, honey and lemon zest with an electric hand whisk until it has tripled in volume and the mixture leaves a thick ribbon trail when you lift the beaters. Add the sifted dry ingredients and whisk lightly. Add the melted butter and fold in until just incorporated.

Spoon the mixture into the prepared pan. You should have about half the mixture remaining – cover with clingfilm/plastic wrap and refrigerate until later. Bake the madeleines in the preheated oven for 15 minutes. Remove from the oven and turn out onto a wire rack to cool.

Wash, butter and flour the madeleine pan, fill with the remaining mixture and bake as before. Eat the first batch whilst waiting for the second to bake! Dust with icing/confectioners' sugar to serve.

The madeleines are best eaten on the day of baking, or can be frozen for up to 2 months.

meringues

Crisp on the outside and chewy in the middle, meringues are so versatile. Their sweet simplicity of flavour combines particularly well with fresh fruit. Make them into nests and top with whipped cream and berries for a delicious dessert, or sandwich shells together for a tasty teatime treat.

3 egg whites
½ teaspoon white vinegar
¼ teaspoon vanilla extract
180g/1 cup caster/superfine sugar

to serve
600 ml/2½ cups whipping cream
30 g/3 tablespoons caster/superfine sugar
fresh fruit of choice

2 baking sheets lined with non-stick baking parchment

Makes about 20

Preheat oven to 110°C (225°F) Gas ¼.

Put the egg whites, vinegar and vanilla into a large, clean, grease-free bowl and whisk on high speed with an electric hand whisk until it has doubled in volume and stiff peaks are formed. Add about a third of the sugar and beat on high speed for 5 minutes until all the sugar is dissolved. Repeat this process, adding the sugar a third at a time and beating for 5 minutes between each addition. The mixture should become stiff.

Scoop spoonfuls of the mixture onto the prepared baking sheets to form mounds of the desired size. Make a dip in each one with the spoon to form a nest shape.

Bake the meringues in the preheated oven for about 60–80 minutes or until they sound crispy and hollow when tapped underneath. Turn off the oven and leave them to cool in the oven with the door ajar for about 30 minutes. Remove from the oven and transfer to a wire rack to cool completely.

To serve, whip the cream and sugar with an electric hand whisk until soft peaks are formed. Serve the meringue nests topped with whipped cream and fresh fruit of your choice.

The meringues will keep for 14 days in an airtight container, or can be frozen for up to 2 months.

traffic light tarts

A great-tasting pastry base and cheery fruit fillings turn the humble jam tart into something rather special. They are perfect for kids' parties, or simply use them to add a tasty bit of colour to your afternoon tea.

1 quantity Pâte Sablée (page 127),
   at room temperature

filling

4 dessertspoons seedless
   raspberry jam

4 dessertspoons apricot conserve

4 dessertspoons lemon and lime
   marmalade

12-hole shallow non-stick
bun pan
9-cm/3½-inch round cookie cutter

Makes 12

Preheat the oven to 180°C (350°F) Gas 4.

Roll out the pastry on a well-floured
surface until 3 mm/⅛ inch thick. Use the
cookie cutter to cut discs of pastry to fit your
bun pan. Not all the pastry will be needed –
the excess will make another 6 or 8 tarts or
can be frozen for future use.

Put the pastry discs in the pan holes and
put a spoonful of jam into each one. Bake the
tarts in the preheated oven for 20–25 minutes.
Remove from the oven and leave to cool in
the pan for 15 minutes before turning out
onto a wire rack to cool completely.

The tarts are best eaten on the day of
baking, or will keep for up to 2 days in an
airtight container.

blueberry & raspberry mini megs

Small is beautiful – and this doesn't just apply to artisan bakeries, it applies to what we make too, it seems. Since we developed Mini Megs, scaled-down versions of some of our most popular cakes, they have very quickly become our best-selling product. They make such a lovely gift, a 'proper cake' but in a portion size that's almost guilt free!

320 g/2⅔ sticks salted butter, soft
320 g/1⅔ cups (caster) sugar
grated zest of 2 large oranges
4 eggs
320 g/2¾ cups plain/all-purpose flour
80 g/½ cup ground almonds
200 g/1½ cups fresh blueberries
200 g/1½ cups fresh raspberries

12 small panettone cases (page 4)

Makes 12

Preheat the oven to 170°C (325°F) Gas 3.

Cream the butter, sugar and orange zest together in a large bowl until pale and fluffy. Add the eggs one at a time, beating well between each addition. Fold in the flour and ground almonds.

Using 2 spoons, divide the mixture equally between the panettone cases, filling each case half full. Arrange the fruit on the surface of each Mini Meg to make 6 of each variety. Bake the cakes in the preheated oven for 45 minutes. A skewer inserted in the middle should come out clean.

The cakes will keep for up to 5 days in an airtight container, or can be frozen for up to 1 month.

banbury cakes

Perhaps best know for the nursery rhyme about 'a fine lady upon a white horse', Banbury is also the home of these special cakes. Thought to date back to the thirteenth century when crusaders brought dried fruit and exotic spices back with them, they could be one of the oldest cake recipes in Britain. Sweet and spicy, they are best eaten warm from the oven.

500 g/16 oz. puff pastry, chilled

120 g/⅔ cup demerara sugar

60 g/½ stick salted butter, cubed

120 g/scant cup raisins

120 g/scant cup Zante currants

60 g/½ cup mixed candied peel, diced

1 teaspoon freshly grated nutmeg

1 teaspoon mixed spice/apple pie spice

75 g/⅓ cup granulated sugar

2 baking sheets lined with baking parchment

Makes 9

Preheat the oven to 200°C (400°F) Gas 6.

Roll out the chilled pastry on a lightly floured surface to a square 3 mm/⅛ inch thick – any thicker and it will rise too much later. Use a knife to cut nine 12-cm/5-inch squares of pastry.

Put the demerara sugar, butter, dried fruit, mixed peel and spices in a large bowl and mix together using your fingers until it binds. Divide the mixture into 9 balls of equal size and place one in the middle of each pastry square. Pull all the opposing corners of each square together and pinch them to join, then repeat this action with the 4 folds that are created. Turn the cakes over and lightly flatten them with the palm of your hand. Gently roll the cakes out into circles about 10 cm/4 inches in diameter and about 1 cm/½ inch thick. Lightly brush the top of each cake with water. Tip the granulated sugar onto a plate and press the dampened side of the cakes into the sugar. Arrange the cakes on the prepared baking sheets, sugar side up, and cut 3 slashes into the top of each one with a sharp knife. Bake them in the preheated oven for 25 minutes, then let cool on the baking sheets.

The cakes are best eaten on the day of baking.

butterfly cakes

Perfect for coffee mornings, village fêtes and an absolute must for children's parties, these pretty cakes look great and are quick and easy to make. Ring the changes by making a selection of flavours; shown below is the recipe for orange, with vanilla and chocolate variations, but you could try coffee, lemon or fish paste. Sorry, couldn't think of a sixth flavour, but you get the idea!

orange butterfly cakes

100 g/6½ tablespoons salted butter, soft

100 g/½ cup (caster) sugar

grated zest of 1 orange

2 eggs

100 g/¾ cup self-raising flour

orange filling

100 g/6½ tablespoons salted butter, soft

200 g/1⅓ cups icing/confectioners' sugar

grated zest of 1 orange, plus the juice of ½ orange

12-hole bun pan, lined with paper cupcake cases

piping bag (optional)

Makes 12

Preheat the oven to 190°C (375°F) Gas 5.

Using an electric hand whisk, cream the butter, sugar, and orange zest together in a large mixing bowl until pale and fluffy. Add the eggs one at a time, beating well between each addition. With the whisk on slow speed, gradually add the flour to achieve a smooth, creamy consistency.

Spoon the mixture into the paper cases and bake in the preheated oven for 12–15 minutes or until golden brown and the tops spring back from light finger pressure. Remove from the oven and transfer to a wire rack to cool.

To make the filling, beat the butter, icing/confectioners' sugar, orange juice and zest together with an electric hand whisk. Start on slow speed and increase to high speed when all the sugar is incorporated, beating for about 2–3 minutes in total.

When cakes have cooled, slice the top off them, then cut each top in half to form wings. Pipe or spoon the buttercream onto the top of the cakes and place the wings on top. Dust icing/confectioners' sugar over them. The cakes are best eaten on the day of baking.

VANILLA VARIATION: Add ¼ teaspoon vanilla extract in place of the orange zest. For the vanilla filling, mix 1 teaspoon vanilla extract and 2 tablespoons water together and add to the butter and sugar in place of the orange juice and zest.

CHOCOLATE VARIATION: Stir 1 tablespoon cocoa powder and 1 tablespoon water together to form a paste and add to the butter and sugar in place of the orange zest. For the chocolate filling, mix 2 tablespoons cocoa powder and 1 tablespoon water together to form a paste and add to butter and sugar in place of orange juice and zest.

brownies
& bars

chocolate fudge brownies

The kind of disappointing, mealy brown cake served in most cafés as brownies is to me a long way from the real thing. A genuine brownie should first and foremost taste of chocolate. There should be undertones of coffee and vanilla and it should be dark and nutty, with a fudge-like centre and a firm, slightly crispy outer surface. This is the original Meg Rivers recipe. Of course I am biased, but I think it can't be bettered.

3 eggs
220 g/1 cup plus 2 tablespoons (caster) sugar
300 g/10 oz. dark/bittersweet chocolate, broken into pieces
220 g/15 tablespoons salted butter
2 tablespoons vanilla extract
1 tablespoon instant coffee powder
2 tablespoons water, boiling
70 g/½ cup self-raising flour
100 g/⅔ cup chopped walnuts

34 x 20 x 3-cm/14 x 8 x 1¼-inch baking pan, lined with baking parchment

Makes 20 portions

Preheat the oven to 180°C (350°F) Gas 4.

Put the eggs and sugar in a large bowl. With a balloon whisk or an electric hand whisk, whisk together until smooth, very thick and pale, and no sugar is left in the base of the bowl.

Melt the chocolate and butter in a heatproof bowl set over a pan of simmering water. Do not let the base of the bowl touch the water. Stir frequently until smooth and well mixed. Put the vanilla extract and coffee powder in a cup, add the boiling water and stir vigorously until dissolved and smooth. Add the melted chocolate and butter to the egg and sugar mix, followed by the coffee infusion and stir to mix. Fold in the flour, then add the walnuts and gently stir through.

Spoon the mixture into the prepared baking pan and bake in the preheated oven for 35–40 minutes until just firm to the touch. Remove the brownies from the oven and let cool in the pan, then turn out onto a wire rack. They are best eaten warm or at room temperature but are easier to slice when chilled. To portion, refrigerate the brownies until chilled, then slice with a sharp knife.

The brownies will keep in an airtight container at room temperature for 7–10 days. They are also good for home freezing.

bakewell slices

If you like Bakewell tart but have only ever eaten the commercially produced variety, you're in for a treat. No sign here of sickly sweet fondant icing or a neon-bright cherry on top – just a sweet pastry base, good raspberry jam and fragrant frangipane paste topped with almonds. It is excellent as a teatime treat or, served warm with cream, it makes a brilliant dessert.

base

1 quantity Pâte Sablée (page 127)

150 g/⅔ cup raspberry jam

filling

130 g/9 tablespoons salted
    butter, soft

160 g/¾ cup (caster) sugar

4 eggs

260 g/1¾ cups ground almonds

40 g/⅓ cup flaked/slivered
    almonds, to decorate

*34 x 20 x 3-cm/14 x 8 x 1¼-inch
    baking pan*

baking parchment

baking beans

Makes 12

Preheat the oven to 170°C (325°F) Gas 3. Remove the Pâte Sablée from the refrigerator and allow to rest at room temperature for 15 minutes before using.

On a lightly floured work surface, carefully roll out the Pâte Sablée until about 5 mm/¼ inch thick and use it to line the baking pan. The pastry is fragile to handle but any gaps can be repaired using surplus pastry. Gently press along the sides and into the corners and trim off the excess pastry with a sharp knife. Prick the base in a few places with a fork and line the tart case with a sheet of baking parchment. Fill the tart case with baking beans and blind bake in the preheated oven for 15–20 minutes. Remove from the oven and set aside to cool. Leave the oven on.

Spread the raspberry jam evenly over the cooled pastry base.

To make the filling, cream together the butter and sugar in a large bowl until pale and fluffy. Add the eggs one at a time, beating after each addition. Add the ground almonds and whisk thoroughly.

Spoon the filling over the jam base and spread to the sides of the pan. Sprinkle the flaked/slivered almonds over the top and bake in the hot oven for 30–35 minutes or until the filling is golden on top and feels firm in the middle. Remove from the oven and allow to cool before cutting into 12 slices.

The slices will keep for 5–7 days in an airtight container.

chocolate, ginger
& orange slices

This recipe is based on our best-selling brownie. We've kept the dense, fudge-like texture but brought an extra dimension to the flavour with the addition of orange and ginger, 2 flavours that complement chocolate beautifully.

3 eggs

220 g/1 cup plus 2 tablespoons (caster) sugar

300 g/10 oz. dark/bittersweet chocolate, broken into pieces

220 g/15 tablespoons salted butter

4½ teaspoons vanilla extract

1 tablespoon instant coffee powder

2 tablespoons water, boiling

finely grated zest of 3 oranges

2 nuggets of stem ginger in syrup, drained and finely chopped

2 teaspoons ground ginger

80 g/⅔ cup self-raising flour

50 g/⅓ cup crystallized ginger, finely diced

34 x 20 x 3-cm/14 x 8 x 1¼-inch baking pan, lined with baking parchment

Makes 14–16

Preheat the oven to 180°C (350°F) Gas 4.

Put the eggs and sugar in a large bowl. With a balloon whisk or an electric hand whisk, whisk together until smooth, very thick and pale, and no sugar is left in the base of the bowl.

Melt the chocolate and butter in a heatproof bowl set over a pan of simmering water. Do not let the base of the bowl touch the water. Stir frequently until smooth and well mixed. Put the vanilla extract and coffee powder in a cup, add the boiling water and stir vigorously until dissolved and smooth. Add the melted chocolate and butter to the beaten egg and sugar mix, followed by the coffee infusion and the orange zest. Stir with a balloon whisk until smooth. Stir in the stem ginger. Sift together the ground ginger and flour, then gently stir into the bowl until well mixed. Spoon the mixture into the prepared baking pan, sprinkle the crystallized ginger evenly over the top and bake in the preheated oven for 35–40 minutes or until just firm to the touch.

Remove the brownies from the oven and let cool in the pan, then turn out onto a wire rack. They are best eaten warm or at room temperature but are easier to slice when chilled. To portion, refrigerate the brownies until chilled, then slice with a sharp knife. The brownies will keep in an airtight container at room temperature for 7–10 days.

flapjacks

Wholesome and nourishing and packed with oats for slow-release energy, a chunk of flapjack will keep you going for hours. Simple, inexpensive and so easy to make, this is a great recipe to get children involved with baking.

330 g/3½ cups jumbo rolled oats

140 g/1½ cups medium rolled oats

100 g/½ cup packed dark muscovado/dark brown sugar

200 g/13 tablespoons salted butter

200 g/¾ cup golden syrup/light corn syrup

50 g/3 tablespoons glucose syrup or liquid glucose (see Tip on page 82)

34 x 20 x 3-cm/14 x 8 x 1¼-inch baking pan, lined with baking parchment

Makes 14–16

Preheat the oven to 180°C (350°F) Gas 4.

In a large bowl, stir together the oats and sugar, crumbling any lumps of sugar with your fingers to ensure it is fully mixed.

In a saucepan set over medium heat, melt together the butter, golden/corn syrup and glucose syrup (if using). Do not allow to boil. Pour into the bowl with the oats and carefully stir together with a wooden spoon – stirring too vigorously at this stage has the effect of making the finished flapjack dense and you'll lose the nice open, crumbly texture.

Spoon the mixture into the prepared baking pan and gently level the top with a fork, easing the mixture along the edges and into the corners. Bake in the preheated oven for 25 minutes or until golden brown. Remove from the oven and let cool in the pan. The flapjack is quite soft at first but hardens as it cools. When completely cool, turn out of the pan onto a board and cut into 14–16 slices with a sharp serrated knife, using a sawing motion.

The flapjacks will keep for 7–10 days in an airtight container.

maggie's muesli bars

When we were asked to supply something to sustain hundreds of fundraisers on an all-night hike through London, we thought we'd better come up with something wholesome and tasty. Made with 2 types of oats for slow-release energy and packed with superfoods like dried apricots, goji berries and cranberries, these yummy cereal bars certainly filled the bill.

135 g/1⅓ cups jumbo rolled oats

135 g/1⅓ cups medium rolled oats

70 g/⅓ cup packed dark muscovado/dark brown sugar

50 g/⅓ cup chopped dried apricots

35 g/¼ cup dried cranberries

35 g/¼ cup pitted and chopped Medjool dates

35 g/¼ cup raisins

35 g/¼ cup dried goji berries

50 g/⅓ cup sunflower seeds

35 g/¼ cup roughly chopped pecans

35g/¼ cup roughly chopped walnuts

35 g/⅓ cup desiccated coconut

200 g/13 tablespoons salted butter

70 g/⅓ cup golden syrup/light corn syrup

40 g/3 tablespoons glucose syrup (or liquid glucose – see Tip opposite)

1 teaspoon vanilla extract

34 x 20 x 3-cm/14 x 8 x 1¼-inch baking pan, lined with baking parchment

Makes 14–16

Preheat the oven to 160°C (325°F) Gas 3.

Put the oats, sugar, dried fruit, sunflower seeds and nuts into a large bowl and mix together with a wooden spoon.

In a saucepan set over low heat, melt together the butter, golden syrup/corn syrup, glucose syrup and vanilla extract, stirring continuously. Alternatively, melt them in short bursts in a microwave, checking and stirring regularly. Pour the melted ingredients over the dry mixture in the bowl and fold together with the wooden spoon.

Spoon the mixture into the prepared baking pan and press the mixture down firmly and evenly using a large metal spoon. Bake in the preheated oven for 35 minutes.

Remove from the oven and allow to cool. When completely cool, turn out of the pan onto a board and cut into 14–16 slices with a sharp serrated knife, using a sawing motion.

Wrap individual slices in clingfilm/plastic wrap and store in an airtight container for 7–10 days.

TIP: Glucose syrup, or liquid glucose, is not essential in this or the Flapjacks recipe on page 81, but it helps give a nice gooey finished texture – if you can't find it, increase the quantity of golden syrup/light corn syrup by the same amount instead.

apricot & orange traybake

Apricots and oranges bring a decidedly summery flavour to this easy-to-make traybake. Fresh apricots are pretty much available year round these days but organic dried ones work well too – you just need to remember to soak them overnight in advance.

150 g/1¼ sticks salted butter, soft

200 g/1 cup (caster) sugar

3 eggs, lightly beaten

finely grated zest of 3 oranges

45 g/⅓ cup plain/all-purpose flour

180 g/1½ cups self-raising flour

6 fresh apricots, halved and pitted

1 tablespoon demerara/raw cane sugar

34 x 20 x 3-cm/14 x 8 x 1¼-inch baking pan, lined with baking parchment

Makes 10 slices

Preheat the oven to 170°C (325°F) Gas 3.

Cream the butter and sugar together in a large bowl until pale and fluffy. Add the beaten eggs in 2 stages, stirring to a smooth batter each time. Stir in the orange zest. Sift the flours together, then add to the mixture and stir to a smooth paste.

Spoon the mixture into the prepared baking pan and spread level with a palette knife. Arrange the apricots, cut side up, on the surface of the mixture and sprinkle the demerara/raw cane sugar evenly over cake. Bake in the preheated oven for about 40 minutes. A skewer inserted in the middle of the cake should come out clean. Remove from the oven and run a knife around the sides of the pan before turning out onto a wire rack. Serve warm.

The traybake will keep, refrigerated, for 3–4 days in an airtight container.

chocolate tiffin

A firm favourite with children, tiffin is a simple, fun-to-make recipe that they'll enjoy helping you with. Using good-quality chocolate, fruit and nuts means this delicious, no-bake cake is equally appealing to adults. Quick and easy to prepare, it can be made in advance and is ideal to serve at parties.

400 g/14 oz. digestive biscuits/graham crackers

100 g/⅔ cup sultanas/golden raisins

70 g/½ cup roughly chopped pecans

60 g/½ cup chopped glacé cherries

70 g/½ cup dark/bittersweet chocolate chips or chunks

250 g/8½ oz. dark/bittersweet chocolate, roughly chopped

90 g/⅓ cup plus 1 tablespoon golden syrup/light corn syrup

70 g/4½ tablespoons unsalted butter

34 x 20 x 3-cm/14 x 8 x 1¼-inch baking pan, lined with baking parchment

Makes 18 portions

Put the biscuits/crackers in a plastic bag and tap them with a rolling pin to break them into small pieces, not crumbs. Put the pieces in a large bowl with the sultanas/golden raisins, pecans, cherries and chocolate chips and mix together with a wooden spoon.

Put the chopped chocolate in a heatproof bowl set over a pan of barely simmering water. Do not let the base of the bowl touch the water. Add the syrup and butter and mix together, stirring continuously, until melted and smooth. This can also be done in a microwave: heat for a few seconds, remove, stir and return to the microwave, repeating until fully melted.

Pour the melted chocolate mixture into the mixing bowl with the dry ingredients and mix until everything is well coated in chocolate.

Spoon the mixture into the prepared baking pan, spread level and press down firmly with the back of the spoon. Refrigerate and allow to harden completely, preferably overnight. To portion, slice using a sharp knife.

The tiffin will keep for 3–5 days in the refrigerator, or freeze for up to 2 months.

parkin pieces

85 g/⅔ cup plain/
all-purpose flour

85 g/¾ cup medium
oatmeal

40 g/3 tablespoons dark
muscovado sugar

1 teaspoon ground ginger

¼ teaspoon grated nutmeg

½ teaspoon bicarbonate
of/baking soda

65 g/½ stick salted butter

60 g/¼ cup golden syrup
/light corn syrup

65 g/¼ cup black treacle/
dark molasses

1 egg, lightly beaten

*18 x 18-cm/7 x 7-inch
baking pan, lined with
baking parchment*

Makes 9

Our Yorkshire parkin uses half treacle and half golden syrup, which gives it a lighter colour and sweeter taste. It gets more delicious over time, so is best baked a week in advance.

Preheat the oven to 170°C (325°F) Gas 3.

Put the flour, oatmeal, sugar, spices and bicarbonate of/baking soda in a large bowl and mix together with your fingertips until all the ingredients, especially the sugar, are thoroughly combined.

In a saucepan set over low heat, melt the butter, syrup and treacle/molasses together until fully liquid.

Slowly add the melted ingredients, the egg and 65 ml/¼ cup warm water to the dry ingredients, stirring rapidly all the time, until a smooth texture is obtained.

Pour the mixture into the prepared baking pan and bake in the preheated oven for 45 minutes or until the surface of the parkin springs back from finger pressure.

When the pan has cooled enough to be safely handled, turn out the parkin and allow to cool fully on a wire rack. Cut into 9 squares, wrap in clingfilm/plastic wrap and place in an airtight container. Store in a cool place (not refrigerated) for 24 hours or so before serving. If you can resist long enough, it will get stickier and more delicious over time! It will keep for up to 2 weeks in an airtight container.

biscuits
& cookies

lemon cookies

These lovely lemon treats are quick and easy to make. They're also great for home freezing, so it's worth baking an extra batch if you have the space.

150 g/1¼ sticks salted butter, firm but not hard

90 g/scant ½ cup (golden caster) sugar

170 g/1⅓ cups self-raising flour

55 g/scant ½ cup plain/all-purpose flour

finely grated zest of 2 lemons

5-cm/2-inch round cookie cutter

baking sheet lined with baking parchment

Makes 18–20

Preheat the oven to 170°C (325°F) Gas 3.

In a large bowl, cream the butter and sugar together until pale and fluffy. Sift the flours into another bowl. Add a quarter of the total flours to the creamed butter and stir in. Add another quarter of the flour and the lemon zest and begin rubbing the mixture together using your fingertips. Add the remaining flour, and mix again with your fingers. Knead gently into a malleable ball of dough. This can also be done by putting all the ingredients in a food processor and blending until it forms a smooth ball of dough.

Put the dough on a lightly floured surface and roll it out until about 1 cm/ ½ inch thick. Stamp out discs with the cookie cutter and arrange them 4 cm/ 1½ inches apart on the prepared baking sheet. Re-roll any leftover dough and cut out cookies, as before, until all the dough is used up. Bake in the preheated oven for 20 minutes, or until the bases of the cookies are golden and the tops are almost firm to the touch. Remove from the oven and allow to cool and set on the baking sheet before eating or storing.

The cookies will keep for 7–10 days in an airtight container or freeze for up to 2 months.

hokey pokey biscuits

This recipe is one we gained from a young New Zealander who came to stay with us one summer. Like Marty, the biscuits soon became a family favourite. Marty described Hokey Pokey biscuits as being 'world famous in New Zealand'. Quick and very easy to make, this is a good recipe to get children involved with.

125 g/1 stick unsalted butter

115 g/½ cup plus 1 tablespoon (caster) sugar

1 generous tablespoon golden syrup/light corn syrup

1 tablespoon milk

175 g/1⅓ cups plus 1 tablespoon plain/all-purpose flour

1 teaspoon baking powder

2 baking sheets (ungreased)

Makes about 20

Preheat the oven to 180°C (350°F) Gas 4.

Put the butter, sugar, syrup and milk in a saucepan. Heat, stirring constantly, until the butter is melted and the mixture is nearly boiling. This can also be done in a microwave: put the ingredients in a bowl and heat in short bursts, stirring between each, until the mixture is ready. Remove from the heat and allow the mixture to cool to lukewarm.

Sift the flour and baking powder together into a large bowl. Pour the butter mixture into the bowl and stir well to combine. Take generous teaspoonfuls of the mix and, with another spoon, drop onto the baking sheets, leaving about 5 cm/2 inches between each biscuit. Lightly press the biscuits with a fork to flatten (dip the fork in a cup of water to prevent it sticking to the dough) and bake in the preheated oven for 15–20 minutes or until golden.

Remove the biscuits from the oven and allow to stand for a few minutes before transferring to a wire rack to cool completely.

The biscuits are best eaten on the day of baking but will keep for 2–3 days in an airtight container.

shortbread

Crisp and buttery, these simple-to-make biscuits have long been a favourite. Meg's recipe uses cornflour/cornstarch for a creamier texture and rice flour to give a crisper bite. You don't mess with the classics – it took us 10 years to decide to add a pinch of salt! There is nothing better to enjoy with a cup of tea, or to serve with whipped cream and fresh strawberries for a lovely summer dessert.

165 g/11 tablespoons salted butter, firm but not hard

85 g/scant ½ cup (caster) sugar

200 g/1½ cups plus 2 tablespoons plain/all-purpose flour

5 teaspoons cornflour/cornstarch

35 g/¼ cup rice flour

a pinch of salt

5-cm/2-inch round cookie cutter

baking sheet lined with baking parchment

Makes 20

Preheat the oven to 170°C (325°F) Gas 3.

In a large bowl, cream the butter and sugar together until pale and fluffy. Sift the flour, cornflour/cornstarch and rice flour into another bowl, then add a quarter of the total flours to the creamed butter and stir in. Add another quarter of the flour and begin rubbing the mixture together using your fingertips. Add the remaining flour and mix again with your fingers. Knead gently into a malleable ball of dough. This can also be done by putting all the ingredients in a food processor and blending until it forms a smooth ball of dough.

Tip the dough out onto a lightly floured surface and roll it out until about 1 cm/½ inch thick (roll a little thinner if you are using the biscuits to make a strawberry dessert). Stamp out discs with the cookie cutter and arrange about 4 cm/1½ inches apart on the prepared baking sheet. Re-roll any leftover dough and cut out discs, as before, until all the dough is used up. Bake in the preheated oven for 20 minutes or until the bases of the biscuits are golden and the tops are almost firm to the touch. Remove the biscuits from the oven and allow them to cool and set on the baking sheet before eating or storing.

The cookies will keep for 7–10 days in an airtight container or freeze for up to 2 months.

macadamia nut biscuits

Macadamia nuts are similar to Brazil nuts (a good substitute) in flavour and texture, and are said to have all kinds of health benefits. It's probably hard to claim that these yummy biscuits are good for you, but they take very little time to make and usually even less time to disappear!

80 g/⅓ cup light muscovado sugar

60 g/½ stick salted butter

80 g/⅓ cup golden syrup/light corn syrup

100 g/¾ cup plain/all-purpose flour

2 teaspoons bicarbonate of/baking soda

80 g/scant ½ cup ground almonds

50 g/⅓ cup shelled macadamia nuts, chopped

4-cm/1½-inch round cookie cutter

baking sheet lined with baking parchment

Makes about 18

Preheat the oven to 180°C (350°F) Gas 4.

Put all the ingredients except the macadamia nuts in a large bowl. Hold the bowl with one hand and use the other hand to bind the ingredients into a paste. Add the chopped nuts and work into the paste in the same manner, forming the mixture into a ball.

Tip the dough out onto a lightly floured surface and roll it out until about 1 cm/½ inch thick. Stamp out biscuits using the cookie cutter and arrange them 4 cm/1½ inches apart on the prepared baking sheet, as they spread quite a bit during baking. Re-roll any leftover dough and cut out biscuits, as before, until all the dough is used up. Bake the biscuits in the preheated oven for about 12–15 minutes or until risen and lightly coloured. Remove the biscuits from the oven and allow them to cool and set on the baking sheet before eating or storing.

The biscuits will keep for 7–10 days in an airtight container or freeze for up to 2 months.

chocolate cookies

This is what you could call a 'grown-up' chocolate cookie – a dark, rugged appearance, satisfyingly crisp bite and such an intense chocolate flavour that they should probably be kept on the top shelf!

125 g/1 stick salted butter, soft

125 g/⅔ cup (caster) sugar

½ teaspoon vanilla extract

155 g/1 cup plus 3 tablespoons plain/all-purpose flour

30 g/2 tablespoons unsweetened cocoa powder

¼ teaspoon baking powder

60 g/½ cup dark/bittersweet chocolate chips or chunks

5-cm/2-inch round cookie cutter

baking sheet lined with baking parchment

Makes about 18

Preheat the oven to 180°C (350°F) Gas 4.

In a large bowl, cream together the butter, sugar and vanilla until pale and fluffy. Add the flour, cocoa powder, baking powder and chocolate chips and mix until a breadcrumb-like consistency is achieved. Vigorously knead the mixture together with your hands to form a ball of dough. This can also be done by putting all the ingredients in a food processor and blending until it forms a smooth ball of dough.

Tip the dough out onto a very lightly floured surface (the dough will be very dry – avoid excess flouring) and roll it out until about 1 cm/½ inch thick. Stamp out discs with the cookie cutter and arrange them 4 cm/1½ inches apart on the prepared baking sheet. Re-roll any leftover dough and cut out cookies, as before, until all the dough is used up. Bake in the preheated oven for 15 minutes, then allow to cool on the sheet. They will harden as they cool. They will keep for 7–10 days in an airtight container or freeze for up to 2 months.

amaretti biscuits

These versatile little almond-flavoured biscuits are crunchy on the outside and chewy on the inside. Perfect to serve with coffee anytime, they also make a great teatime treat when sandwiched together with buttercream, or serve them with the best coffee or vanilla ice cream as a dessert.

2 egg whites

175 g/¾ cup plus 2 tablespoons (caster) sugar

200 g/1⅓ cups ground almonds

1 tablespoon Amaretto liqueur

30 whole shelled almonds, to decorate

piping bag fitted with a 12-mm/ ½-inch nozzle/tip (optional)

2 baking sheets lined with baking parchment

Makes about 30

Preheat the oven to 170°C (325°F) Gas 3.

In a clean, grease-free bowl, whisk the egg whites using an electric hand whisk until firm peaks are formed. Add the sugar, ground almonds and Amaretto and gently fold into the egg whites until you have a smooth paste.

Fill the piping bag (if using) with the mixture and squeeze approximate 4-cm/1½-inch circles onto the prepared baking sheets. This can also be done using 2 dessertspoons – one to scoop the mixture from the bowl and the other to scrape it off onto the baking sheet. Place a whole almond in the centre of each biscuit and bake in the preheated oven for 20 minutes or until risen, pale golden and they have small cracks over the surface. Remove the biscuits from the oven and allow them to cool on the baking sheet.

The biscuits will keep for 7–10 days in an airtight container.

ginger biscuits

Hot and spicy, these delicious biscuits are ideal for dunking. Teamed with the Ginger Cake recipe on page 28 and packed in a pretty tin, they make a great gift for any ginger lover.

90 g/⅓ cup plus 1 tablespoon golden syrup/light corn syrup

65 g/½ stick salted butter

90 g/½ cup dark muscovado/dark brown sugar

1 large nugget of stem ginger in syrup, finely chopped

20 ml/1½ tablespoons milk

200 g/1½ cups plain/all-purpose flour

2 teaspoons bicarbonate of/baking soda

2½ teaspoons ground ginger

2½ teaspoons mixed spice/apple pie spice

baking sheet lined with baking parchment

Makes about 24

Preheat the oven to 190°C (375°F) Gas 5.

Melt the syrup, butter and sugar in a saucepan set over low heat, stirring continuously. This can also be done in a microwave: put the ingredients in a heatproof bowl in the microwave for about 15 seconds, remove from the microwave and stir to check the consistency. Repeat as necessary.

Add the chopped stem ginger to the mixture, followed by the milk, and stir to combine.

Sift the flour, bicarbonate of/baking soda and spices into a mixing bowl, pour the melted ingredients on top and stir until smooth. Chill until the mixture becomes firm enough to handle.

Turn the dough out onto a lightly floured surface and roll into walnut-sized balls. Arrange the balls 5 cm/2 inches apart on the prepared baking sheet, then press flat with a fork until about 1 cm/½ inch thick (dip the fork in a cup of water to prevent it sticking to the dough). Bake the biscuits in the preheated oven for 12–15 minutes.

If you like your ginger biscuits chewy, eat them fresh from the oven while they're still warm. For a crisp biscuit, allow to cool completely on a wire rack.

The biscuits will keep for 7–10 days in an airtight container or freeze for up to 2 months.

florentines

These chewy and delicious Italian biscuits, full of fruit and nuts with chocolate-coated bases, are great to serve with after-dinner coffee or to crumble over ice cream. They also make a delightfully different edible gift.

50 g/⅓ cup whole glacé cherries

50 g/⅓ cup mixed candied peel

100 g/⅔ cup sultanas/golden raisins

200 g/1½ cups flaked/slivered almonds

50 g/6 tablespoons plain/all-purpose flour

120 g/1 stick salted butter

160 g/¾ cup (caster) sugar

50 ml/3 tablespoons single/light cream

200 g/6½ oz. dark/bittersweet chocolate, roughly chopped

baking sheets lined with baking parchment

5-cm/2-inch round cookie cutter (optional)

Makes about 30

Preheat the oven to 170°C (325°F) Gas 3.

Wash all the syrup from the glacé cherries, dry thoroughly and dice finely. If the pieces of mixed peel are large, dice these the same size as the cherries. Place the diced cherries, mixed peel, sultanas/golden raisins, flaked/slivered almonds and flour in a large bowl.

In a saucepan set over low heat, melt the butter and sugar together. Remove from the heat and stir in the cream, then add this to the ingredients in the bowl. Stir until evenly blended. Spoon 6 walnut-sized scoops of the mixture onto each baking sheet, spaced well apart, gently pressing down the mounds with the back of the spoon. Bake in the preheated oven for 15 minutes or until golden. Remove from the oven and immediately re-shape the florentines into circles – a cookie cutter is ideal for this, or you can use a knife. Transfer to a wire rack to cool and repeat the process until all the mixture is used and baked.

Melt the chocolate in a heatproof bowl set over a pan of barely simmering water. Do not let the base of the bowl touch the water. Remove from the heat and allow to cool, stirring occasionally, until it has thickened to a spreading consistency. Brush some melted chocolate on the underside of each florentine using a pastry brush and leave to set.

The florentines will keep for 7–10 days in an airtight container or freeze for up to 2 months.

loaves
& breads

carrot cake

Moist and wholesome with a pleasant sweetness, there's something honest and comforting about freshly-baked carrot cake.

Preheat the oven to 170°C (325°F) Gas 3.

Put the sugar, egg and corn oil in a large bowl and lightly beat together. Add the flour, baking powder, cinnamon, nutmeg and salt and stir to a smooth mixture. Add the mashed banana, walnuts and sultanas/golden raisins, followed by the carrot, and stir together.

Spoon the mixture into the prepared loaf pan and bake in the preheated oven for 55 minutes. A skewer inserted into the middle of the cake should come out clean. Remove from the oven and allow to cool in the pan for about 15 minutes, then turn out onto a wire rack to cool completely.

To make the topping, put the mascarpone, icing/confectioners' sugar and butter into a bowl and whisk until light and creamy. If desired, add a squeeze of lemon or lime juice to bring a bit of zing to the frosting. Spread the topping over the cake and garnish with lemon zest.

This cake will keep for 5–7 days in the refrigerator.

150 g/¾ cup packed light brown soft sugar

1 egg

170 ml/¾ cup corn oil

140 g/1 cup plus 1½ tablespoons wholemeal/whole-wheat flour

½ teaspoon baking powder

1 teaspoon ground cinnamon

½ teaspoon freshly grated nutmeg

¼ teaspoon salt

1 banana, mashed

50 g/⅓ cup chopped walnuts

30 g/3 tablespoons sultanas/ golden raisins

125 g/⅔ cup grated carrots

topping

100 g/scant ½ cup mascarpone

40 g/⅓ cup icing/confectioners' sugar

10 g/2 teaspoons salted butter, soft

a squeeze of lemon or lime juice (optional)

grated lemon zest, to garnish

500-g/1-lb. loaf pan lined with a paper loaf-pan liner

Serves 8

bara brith

Bara brith is literally translated from the Welsh as 'speckled bread', though no yeast is required. This tasty tea bread was always popular and sold out quickly whenever we attended county shows and farmers' markets. It is best served warmed or toasted and spread with plenty of butter.

2 tea bags

130 ml/½ cup water, boiling

100 g/½ cup packed dark brown sugar

75 g/½ cup Zante currants

75 g/½ cup sultanas/golden raisins

180 g/1½ cups self raising flour

½ teaspoon mixed spice/apple pie spice

½ teaspoon ground cinnamon

¼ teaspoon ground ginger

1 egg

500-g/1-lb. loaf pan lined with a paper loaf-pan liner

Serves about 10

Start the bara brith the day before you want to serve it.

Put the tea bags and boiling water into a jug/pitcher and allow to stand for 15 minutes before removing the tea bags.

Put the sugar, currants and sultanas/golden raisins into a large bowl, add the tea and stir together. Cover with a tea towel and allow to stand and infuse overnight.

The next day, preheat the oven to 170°C (325°F) Gas 3.

Add the flour, spices and egg to the fruit and tea mixture and mix until well combined.

Spoon the mixture into the prepared pan and bake in the preheated oven for 1 hour. Remove from the oven, cover the loaf with foil and bake for a further 15 minutes or until a skewer inserted into the middle of the loaf comes out clean. Allow to cool on a wire rack. Serve thickly spread with butter.

This loaf will keep for 4–5 days in an airtight container.

apricot & nut loaf

This fat-free, fruit and nut loaf was always a favourite at Meg's original tearoom. Back in the day, it was all starched tablecloths and bone china, and we'd serve this loaf, thinly sliced, with pots of Earl Grey tea. We're a bit funkier at the new Meg River's café – not a doily in sight – and this wholesome and nutritious loaf is bang up to date.

60 g/½ cup wholemeal/
    whole-wheat flour
30 g/3 tablespoons ground almonds
160 g/¾ cup packed dark brown sugar
140 g/1 cup sultanas/golden raisins
120 g/1 cup chopped dried apricots
75 g/½ cup chopped mixed nuts
2 eggs, lightly beaten

topping
10 whole dried apricots
50 g/3 tablespoons apricot jam

*500-g/1-lb. loaf pan lined with
    a paper loaf-pan liner*

Serves 20

Preheat the oven to 150°C (300°F) Gas 2.

Put the flour, ground almonds, sugar, sultanas/golden raisins, chopped apricots and nuts in a large bowl and mix together. Add the beaten eggs and stir well.

Spoon the mixture into the prepared loaf pan, smooth level and top with the whole dried apricots. Bake in the preheated oven for 1 hour. A skewer inserted into the cake should come out clean. Remove from the oven and allow to cool in the pan.

Boil the apricot jam in a small saucepan and carefully pour over the top of the loaf to glaze it. When completely cool, remove the loaf from the pan. Serve in thin slices.

The loaf will keep for up to 14 days wrapped in clingfilm/plastic wrap and sealed in an airtight container.

VARIATION: To make a Date & Nut Loaf, simply replace the dried apricots in both the cake and the topping with the same quantity of pitted dates.

lavender loaf

Lavender has been used for centuries as a flavouring for food, and it takes just a tiny amount to transform this simple cake into a delicately flavoured delight, perfect for summer eating.

130 g/1 stick plus 2 teaspoons salted butter, soft

130 g/⅔ cup (caster) sugar

2 eggs

grated zest of 1 lemon

35 g/3 tablespoons ground almonds

100 g/¾ cup plain/all-purpose flour

40 g/⅓ cup self-raising flour

3 teaspoons dried lavender flowers (see Tip below)

500-g/1-lb. loaf pan lined with a paper loaf-pan liner

Serves about 8

Preheat the oven to 170°C (325°F) Gas 3.

In a large bowl, cream the butter and sugar together until pale and fluffy. Add the eggs one at a time, beating between each addition. Add the lemon zest, ground almonds and flours and beat to a smooth batter. Finally, add the lavender and stir through.

Spoon the mixture into the prepared loaf pan, spread level and bake in the preheated oven for 40 minutes. A skewer inserted into the middle of the loaf should come out clean. Remove from the oven and leave to cool in the pan for 30 minutes before turning out onto a wire rack to cool completely.

This cake is best eaten on the day of baking, but will keep for up to 4 days in an airtight container or frozen for up to 2 months.

TIP: If using home-grown lavender, be sure to wash it thoroughly and dry in a low oven. Alternatively, you can buy it from Snowshill Lavender or Fox's Spices; or at www.thefrenchybee.com

fruit bread

This traditional favourite is so simple to make and makes a delicious teatime treat that actually tastes better a day or 2 after baking. Serve it thickly spread with butter and accompanied by a cup of your favourite tea. It is equally delicious toasted.

35 g/2½ tablespoons salted butter, soft

65 g/⅓ cup packed dark brown sugar

1 egg

1 tablespoon black treacle/dark molasses

165 g/1⅓ cups self-raising flour

a pinch of salt

¼ teaspoon mixed spice/apple pie spice

¼ teaspoon ground cinnamon

65 g/½ cup sultanas/golden raisins

25 g/3 tablespoons chopped pecans

500-g/1-lb. loaf pan lined with a paper loaf-pan liner

Serves about 8

Preheat the oven to 170°C (325°F) Gas 3.

In a large bowl, cream the butter and sugar together until paler and fluffy. Add the egg and beat in.

In a separate bowl, combine 90 ml/6 tablespoons warm water and the treacle/molasses, then add to the creamed butter and stir to mix. Sift together the flour, salt and spices. Add to the bowl, followed by the sultanas/golden raisins and pecans, and beat to a smooth mixture.

Spoon the mixture into the prepared loaf pan and bake in the preheated oven for 40–45 minutes or until the top springs back from light finger pressure or a skewer inserted into the middle of the loaf comes out clean.

The bread is best stored overnight and then served spread with butter. It will keep for up to 5 days in an airtight container.

banana & walnut bread

There's no need to waste those excess bananas in future! Economical and easy to make, this moist bread tastes all the better for using over-ripe fruit. It's a flexible recipe too; you can use dried fruit in place of the walnuts or even just leave it plain. Just slice and serve spread with butter, or try it toasted for a tasty change at breakfast.

1 large or 2 small bananas, peeled (over-ripe give best flavour)

40 g/3 tablespoons salted butter, soft

100 g/¾ cup self-raising flour

70 g/⅓ cup (caster) sugar

a pinch of salt

1 egg

100 g/⅔ cup chopped walnuts

500-g/1-lb. loaf pan lined with a paper loaf-pan liner

Serves 8

Preheat the oven to 150°C (300°F) Gas 2.

In a large bowl, mash the banana with a fork. Add the butter, flour, sugar and salt and stir together. Add the egg, followed by the walnuts, and beat into the mixture. This can also be done with an electric stand mixer or hand whisk.

Spoon the mixture into the prepared loaf pan, spread level and bake in the preheated oven for 45 minutes. A skewer inserted into the middle of the loaf should come out clean.

This loaf is best eaten within a day or 2 of baking, but will keep for up to 4 days in an airtight container.

stollen

This spicy bread flavoured with nutmeg, cloves and rum has a sweet surprise in the form of a marzipan centre. It's become increasingly popular in recent years as an alternative to rich fruit Christmas cakes. It can be a bit time-consuming but is not at all difficult to make. If you're going to devote the time to make stollen you might as well make enough. This recipe makes 2 large loaves; one to eat and one to freeze or give away.

melted butter, to glaze
icing/confectioner's sugar, to dust

dough

200 g/13 tablespoons salted butter
600 g/4⅔ cups strong/bread flour
60 g/2 oz. fresh yeast
270 ml/1 cup plus 2 tablespoons milk, warmed
100 g/½ cup (caster) sugar

filling

400 g/14 oz. marzipan
60 g/½ cup chopped almonds
200 g/1⅓ cups raisins
120 g/scant cup Zante currants
120 g/scant cup mixed candied peel, diced
¼ teaspoon grated nutmeg
¼ teaspoon ground cloves
1 tablespoon rum

baking sheet lined with baking parchment

Makes 2 large loaves

To make the dough, melt the butter in a small saucepan and set aside to cool. Sift the flour into a large bowl, crumble in the yeast, add the milk and sugar and knead into a silky dough. This can also be done in an electric stand mixer with a dough hook attachment. Pour the cooled butter over the dough, cover with a clean tea towel and allow to rise for 1 hour.

In the meantime, halve the marzipan and roll out to form 2 ropes, each 25 cm/10 inches long. In a separate bowl, mix together the almonds, raisins, currants, mixed peel, nutmeg, cloves and rum.

When the dough has finished rising, work in the butter. This is very messy and makes the dough very loose at first, but it firms up again as the butter is worked in. Add the fruit, spice and nut mixture and work into the dough.

Turn the dough out onto a lightly floured surface and cut in half. Roll out half of the dough to form a rectangle measuring 25 x 15 cm/10 x 6 inches and place a marzipan rope in the centre. Roll the dough around the marzipan like a Swiss/jelly roll and place on the prepared baking sheet with the seam at the base. Repeat with the other half of the dough. Cover both loaves with a clean tea towel and let stand for an hour in a warm place. After 45 minutes, preheat the oven to 200°C (400°F) Gas 6.

Bake the loaves in the middle of the preheated oven for 35 minutes. Remove from the oven and brush a little melted butter over them. Allow to cool, then dust icing/confectioners' sugar over the top.

The stollen will keep for 2–3 days wrapped in baking foil and sealed in an airtight container. It can be frozen for up to 1 month.

tarts

pâte sucrée

French for 'sweet dough', this is a crisp, sweet pastry ideal for fruit tarts or pies. It is easy to make and freezes well.

320 g/2 sticks plus 5 tablespoons
    salted butter, chilled and cubed
160 g/¾ cup (caster) sugar
500 g/4 cups plain/all-purpose
    flour
1 egg

Makes about 1 kg/2 lbs.

Put the butter, sugar and flour in a large bowl and rub between your fingertips until the texture resembles fine breadcrumbs. (You can add orange or lemon zest at this point if desired.) Add the egg and work the mixture with your hands to a smooth paste.

Wrap the dough in clingfilm/plastic wrap and refrigerate for about 30 minutes until firm.

pâte sablée

This rich, buttery pastry has a crumbly texture that is a little bit difficult to work with, but has such a wonderful, melt-in-the-mouth texture that is worth the extra effort.

200 g/1½ cups plus 2 tablespoons plain/all-purpose flour

50 g/⅓ cup ground almonds

75 g/⅓ cup (caster) sugar

160 g/11 tablespoons salted butter, at room temperature, cubed

1 egg yolk

Makes about 500 g/1 lb.

Put the flour, ground almonds and sugar in a large bowl and stir until evenly mixed. Add the butter and use your fingertips to rub it into the mixture until the texture resembles breadcrumbs. Add the egg yolk and, still using your hands, mix and knead until the dough binds together into a tight, smooth ball – it can seem like it will never bind, but have patience, it will!

Wrap the dough in clingfilm/plastic wrap and refrigerate for about 30 minutes until firm. Before use, remove from the refrigerator and allow to stand at room temperature for 10–15 minutes.

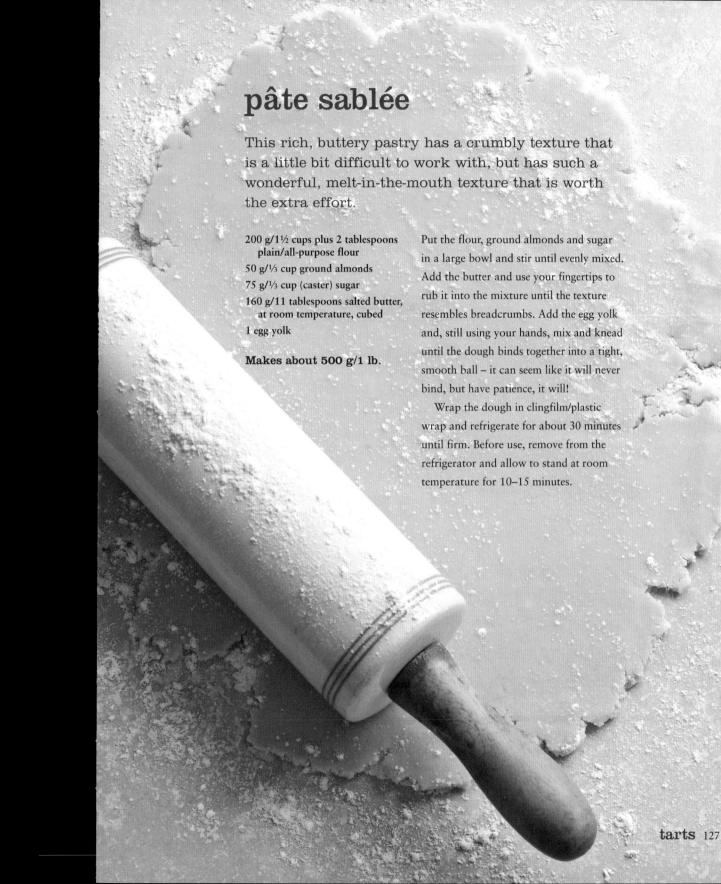

tarte au citron

This classic French-style dessert is so popular at our Cotswold café that it's practically a permanent fixture on the menu. Simple and easy to make, it has a satisfyingly subtle lemon flavour and a wonderful melt-in-the-mouth, creamy texture.

1 quantity Pate Sablée (page 127 but you won't need all of it, so freeze any excess for another time), chilled

filling

3 eggs, plus 1 egg yolk

150 g/¾ cup (caster) sugar

135 ml/½ cup plus 1 tablespoon double/heavy cream

grated zest and freshly squeezed juice of 3 lemons

icing/confectioners' sugar, to dust (optional)

23-cm/9-inch loose-based fluted tart pan

baking parchment

baking beans

chef's blowtorch (optional)

Serves 10–12

Preheat the oven to 190°C (375°F) Gas 5.

Roll out the chilled pastry on a lightly floured surface to form a circle about 30 cm/12 inches in diameter and about 3 mm/⅛ inch thick. Drape the pastry over the rolling pin and carefully transfer it to the tart pan. Gently mould the pastry into the base and sides. The pastry is fragile to handle but any gaps can be repaired using surplus pastry. Trim the top edge with a sharp knife. Prick the base in a few places with a fork and line the tart case with a sheet of baking parchment. Fill the tart case with baking beans and blind bake in the preheated oven for 15–20 minutes. Take out of the oven, remove the baking parchment and baking beans and return to the oven for another 5 minutes to lightly colour the pastry. Remove from the oven and reduce the oven temperature to 180°C (350°F) Gas 4.

To make the filling, put the eggs, egg yolk, sugar, cream and lemon zest and juice into a large bowl. Lightly whisk, then transfer to a saucepan set over low–medium heat. Heat gently, stirring constantly, until starts to thicken. Be careful not to over heat otherwise it can curdle. Put the tart pan on a baking sheet and carefully pour the filling into the tart case. Bake for 15 minutes or until just set. Allow to cool completely before removing from the tart pan. If you choose, you can lightly brown the surface of tart using a chef's blowtorch or simply dust with icing/confectioners' sugar before serving.

Well wrapped, the tart will keep for 3–5 days in the refrigerator.

tarte tatin

It's a bit of a performance to make this classic French upside-down dessert, but well worth the effort. The caramelized fruit and sweet pastry combine to give an irresistible taste. This version uses apples, but pears, prunes or apricots work equally well. A pan capable of withstanding both stovetop and oven is a must. Serve the tart warm with crème fraîche or good vanilla ice cream.

1 quantity Pate Sucrée (page 126, but you won't need all of it, so freeze any excess for another time), at room temperature

filling

4–6 apples, peeled, cored and quartered

70 g/5 tablespoons salted butter

140 g/¾ cup (caster) sugar

½ teaspoon ground cinnamon

24-cm/10-inch flameproof tart pan or heavy-based, ovenproof omelette pan

Serves 8

Preheat the oven to 180°C (350°F) Gas 4.

To make the filling, put the butter, sugar and 1 tablespoon water in the flameproof tart pan or heavy-based, ovenproof omelette pan over low heat. Heat, stirring occasionally, and when the mixture begins to give off a lovely caramel scent and turns golden, remove from the heat (this can take up to 10 minutes). Arrange the apples in the caramel in concentric circles, curved side down. Take extra care at this stage and as a safety precaution have a bowl of cold water ready to dip fingers in, should any hot caramel stick to them.

Return the pan to the heat. Allow to simmer gently for about 15 minutes, watching the pan carefully to ensure the heat is not too high, which can cause the apples to stick to the pan and burn. Remove from the heat when the apples are soft and well soaked in caramel.

Roll out the pastry on a lightly floured surface to form a circle about 5 cm/2 inches larger than the pan and about 4 mm/⅛ inch thick. Carefully place the pastry over the caramelized apples, and pinch the edges to the outside of the pan. Bake in the preheated oven for 35–40 minutes until the pastry turns golden brown. Remove from the oven and trim the excess pastry from the outside of the dish. Allow to stand for 5 minutes. Cover the pan with a serving plate. Ensuring your wrists are protected from any splashes of caramel, grip the plate and dish firmly together and turn them over so that the plate is on the bottom. Give it a gentle shake before carefully lifting the pan clear of the plate. The tart is best eaten on the day of baking but will keep for 2–3 days.

pear tart

Not just a great looking dish, this lovely dessert has it all – buttery pastry, warm frangipane filling and softly yielding fruit. It works with most types of pear, though Comice are particularly good. It can be eaten cold but is hard to beat served warm with cream.

1 quantity Pâte Sablée (page 127 but you won't need all of it, so freeze any excess for another time), chilled

apricot jam, to glaze (optional)

frangipane

65 g/½ stick salted butter, soft

75 g/⅓ cup (caster) sugar

2 eggs

125 g/scant cup ground almonds

4 large pears, halved lengthways

23-cm/9-inch loose-based fluted tart pan

Serves 8–10

Preheat the oven to 170°C (325°F) Gas 3.

Roll out the chilled pastry on a lightly floured surface to form a circle about 30 cm/12 inches in diameter and about 3 mm/⅛ inch thick. Drape the pastry over the rolling pin and carefully transfer it to the tart pan. Gently mould the pastry into the base and sides. The pastry is fragile to handle but any gaps can be repaired using surplus pastry. Trim the top edge with a sharp knife.

To make the frangipane, put the butter and sugar in a large bowl and cream together to a light texture. Beat in the eggs one at a time until the mixture is thoroughly blended. Add the ground almonds and fold in until a smooth, even texture. Spoon into the tart case and spread level with a palette knife.

Using a melon baller or teaspoon, scoop the pips out of the pear halves and discard. Arrange the pears in a circle on top of the frangipane, curved side up. Bake in the preheated oven for about 1 hour or until the frangipane springs back from light finger pressure. Remove from the oven and allow to cool.

Boil a little apricot jam and brush it over the tart to glaze. The tart is best eaten on the day of baking.

pecan & chocolate tart
with maple syrup

Genuine maple syrup has a unique kind of sweetness that adds something extra to this rather decadent dish. Best saved for a special occasion, it's very rich and a little goes a long way.

1 quantity Pate Sucrée (page 126), chilled

filling

200 g/¾ cup maple syrup

20 g/1½ cups muscovado sugar

20 g/1½ tablespoons salted butter

80 g/2½ oz. dark/bittersweet chocolate, finely chopped

3 eggs

150 g/1 cup pecan halves

23-cm/9-inch loose-based fluted tart pan

baking beans

Serves 10–12

Preheat the oven to 190°C (375°F) Gas 5.

Roll out the chilled pastry, line the tart pan and blind bake following the method on page 128. Remove from the oven and reduce the oven temperature to 150°C (300°F) Gas 2.

To make the filling, put maple syrup, sugar and butter into a saucepan and stir over medium heat until melted. Remove from the heat and add the chocolate, stirring until it has melted and the mixture is smooth. Add the eggs and beat into the mixture. Finally, stir in the nuts.

Pour the mixture into the tart case and bake in the preheated oven for 30–35 minutes or until the filling is just set.

The tart can be served warm or at room temperature. It will keep for 2–3 days in an airtight container.

rhubarb & mascarpone tart

Few things can compete with the first cut of outdoor-grown rhubarb every season – the pleasing sharpness of the fruit contrasts wonderfully well with the creamy mascarpone filling in this tart.

filling

500 g/1 lb. rhubarb, cut into 2-cm/1-inch slices

175 g/¾ cup (caster) sugar

30 g/2 tablespoons salted butter, soft

225 g/scant cup mascarpone

30 g/¼ cup plain/all-purpose flour

grated zest of 1 orange

2 eggs, separated

100 ml/scant ½ cup double/heavy cream

shortbread base

135 g/9 tablespoons salted butter, soft

65 g/⅓ cup (caster) sugar

160 g/1¼ cups plain/all-purpose flour

15 g/2 tablespoons cornflour/cornstarch

25 g/3 tablespoons rice flour

syrup

2 teaspoons arrowroot

freshly squeezed juice of 1 orange

23-cm/9-inch loose-based tart pan

baking parchment

baking beans

Serves 8–10

Preheat the oven to 190°C (375°F) Gas 5.

Put the rhubarb for the filling in an ovenproof dish, sprinkle 60 g/⅓ cup of the sugar over the top and cover with foil. Roast in the preheated oven for about 15 minutes. Remove the rhubarb from the oven and strain it, reserving the juice for later. Set aside. Leave the oven on.

To make the shortbread base, put all the ingredients in a large bowl and rub together using your fingertips until it forms a paste. Knead gently into a smooth ball of dough (refrigerate it for a few minutes if it is too soft to work). Alternatively, put the ingredients in the bowl of a food processor or electric stand mixer and blend until it forms a smooth ball of dough. Roll out the pastry on a lightly floured surface to form a circle about 5 cm/ 2 inches larger than the pan. Drape the pastry over the rolling pin and carefully transfer it to the tart pan. Gently mould the pastry into the base and sides. Trim the top edge with a sharp knife. Line the tart case with a sheet of baking parchment. Fill the tart case with baking beans and blind bake in the preheated oven for 15–20 minutes. Take out of the oven, remove the baking parchment and baking beans. When cool, lines the sides of the tart pan with strips of baking parchment about 5 cm/2 inches high.

To make the filling, put the butter, remaining sugar, the mascarpone, flour and orange zest into a large bowl. Beat until evenly mixed, then add the egg yolks and cream. Beat to a creamy consistency and set aside.

Put the egg whites in a clean, grease-free bowl and, using an electric stand mixer or hand whisk, whisk the egg whites on high speed until light and foamy and soft peaks are formed. Transfer to the mascarpone mixture and whisk together, then spoon into the tart case. Distribute the roasted rhubarb evenly over the filling. Bake for 40–45 minutes or until golden brown and the filling is set like a hot soufflé – firm but with a slight wobble!

To make the syrup, stir together the arrowroot and 2 tablespoons water in a cup. Put the reserved rhubarb juice and the orange juice into a saucepan and bring to the boil. Remove from the heat and start stirring in the arrowroot – it may not all be needed, depending on how much juice you've produced from your rhubarb. The syrup should be just slightly thickened, as it thickens further with cooling.

Serve the tart warm with the syrup poured on top.

treacle tart

This is such a nostalgia trip; a good old-fashioned British dessert. Made with what my mother would call 'fancy French pastry' and zest of lemon, it is a bit posher than the version she used to make. Don't tell her, but I reckon it's even more delicious than the ones I remember from childhood.

1 quantity Pâte Sablée (page 127 but you won't need all of it, so freeze any excess for another time), chilled

filling

100 g/1 cup breadcrumbs

60 g/½ cup ground almonds

1 egg, lightly beaten

125 ml/½ cup single/light cream

a pinch of ground ginger

grated zest of 1 lemon

340 g/1½ cups golden syrup/light corn syrup

25 g/½ cup corn flakes, crushed

23-cm/9-inch loose-based fluted tart pan

baking beans

Serves 8–10

Preheat the oven to 190°C (375°F) Gas 5.

Roll out the chilled pastry on a lightly floured surface to form a circle about 30 cm/12 inches in diameter and about 3 mm/⅛ inch thick. Drape the pastry over the rolling pin and carefully transfer it to the tart pan. Gently mould the pastry into the base and sides. The pastry is fragile to handle but any gaps can be repaired using surplus pastry. Trim the top edge with a sharp knife. Line the tart case with a sheet of baking parchment. Fill the tart case with baking beans and blind bake in the preheated oven for 15–20 minutes. Take out of the oven, remove the baking parchment and baking beans and return to the oven for another 5 minutes to lightly colour the pastry. Remove from the oven and reduce the oven temperature to 160°C (325°F) Gas 3.

To make the filling, put the breadcrumbs, ground almonds, egg, cream, ginger and lemon zest into a large bowl and stir together. Warm the syrup in a saucepan, then add it to the mixture in the bowl and blend together.

Spoon the mixture into the tart case, place the tart on a baking sheet and bake in the preheated oven for 20 minutes. Remove from the oven and sprinkle the corn flakes over the tart. Return to the oven and bake for a further 30 minutes. Remove from the oven and allow to cool in the pan.

The tart will keep for up to 7 days in an airtight container.

fig & marsala crostata

I was very tempted to call this recipe Fig & Fennel Flan, but it sounded too silly to do this beautiful Italian tart justice. Marsala is a fortified wine that combines perfectly with dried figs to make a superbly flavoured filling (though if you don't have it to hand, sherry or port work well) but the real surprise is the extra dimension a single teaspoon of fennel seeds added to the pastry brings; it simply lifts the taste experience to a whole new level.

1 teaspoon fennel seeds

1 quantity Pâte Sucrée (page 126 but follow the method here)

filling

550 g/18 oz. dried figs, roughly chopped

440 ml/1¾ cups Marsala

40 g/3 tablespoons dark brown sugar

2 cinnamon sticks

a pinch of ground cloves

23-cm/9-inch loose-based tart pan

Serves 8–10

To make the filling, put 1¾ cups water and the remaining ingredients in a large saucepan set over medium heat and bring to the boil. Turn down the heat and simmer for 40 minutes or until the liquid has reduced by at least half. Remove from the heat and allow to cool slightly.

Remove the cinnamon sticks, then pour the mixture into a food processor and blend for no more than 10 seconds – you don't want a purée, more of a sticky paste. Refrigerate until chilled and thickened.

Meanwhile, to make the pastry, bruise the fennel seeds with a pestle and mortar to release the flavour. If you don't have pestle and mortar, place the fennel in a basin and bruise with the back of a spoon. Using the recipe for Pâte Sucrée on page 126, stir the bruised fennel seeds into the butter, sugar and flour and continue the recipe to complete the pastry. Divide the pastry in half, wrap in clingfilm/plastic wrap and refrigerate for 15 minutes. You won't need all of it, so freeze one half for another time.

Preheat the oven to 170°C (325°F) Gas 3.

Roll out the chilled pastry on a lightly floured surface to form a circle about 30 cm/12 inches in diameter and about 3 mm/⅛ inch thick. Drape the pastry over the rolling pin and carefully transfer it to the tart pan. Gently mould the pastry into the base and sides. The pastry is fragile to handle but any gaps can be repaired using surplus pastry. Trim the top edge with a sharp knife. Reserve any surplus pastry for decoration.

Spoon the chilled filling into the tart case and spread level with a palette knife. Roll out the reserved pastry and cut into 1-cm/½-inch wide strips. Weave the pastry strips in a lattice pattern across the surface of the filling. Place the tart on a baking sheet and bake in the preheated oven for 45–55 minutes or until golden brown. Remove from the oven and allow to cool slightly in the pan.

The tart is lovely served warm with Greek yogurt but it is possibly even nicer cold, the day after baking, once the flavours have had time to develop.

index

acknowledgments

I'd like to say thank you to all the people who helped in getting this book completed.

Firstly to Harriet Griffey who had the idea of a Meg Rivers recipe book and who would not stop pestering me – sorry, encouraging me – until it became a reality. A special thanks goes to all at Meg Rivers, particularly Mike Wallace, head baker, and his second in command, my Number 2 Daughter Felicity Day, for doing all the hard work in perfecting the recipes. Thanks also to Alice Wragg, Number 3 Daughter, who covered my work at the bakery with her usual cheerful efficiency when I was desperately trying to meet the deadline for this book. Thanks also to Céline Hughes and all at RPS for their patience and advice and flexible attitude regarding that deadline! Steve Painter's design and photography are a delight, as is Lucy Mckelvie's beautiful food styling – thank you both. Jane Milton and her team at Not Just Food tested every recipe expertly and were always positive and accurate in their comments. My friend Amanda Wilson was as generous as always with her expertise and experience. Very many thanks to Cath Kidston for her kind endorsement.

Thanks to remaining daughters, Jessica and Nancy, for their encouragement and forthright opinions! Particular thanks to my partner Edith Comby Pigeon for her unending patience and constant support throughout.